PUBLIC SCHOOLS
PRIVATE ENTERPRISE

PUBLIC SCHOOLS

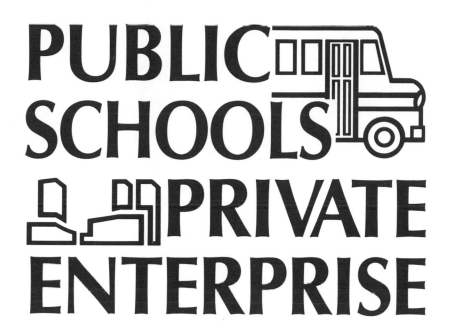

PRIVATE ENTERPRISE

What You Should Know and Do About Privatization

SAMUEL FLAM, Ed.D.
WILLIAM G. KEANE, Ed.D.

TECHNOMIC
PUBLISHING CO., INC.
LANCASTER · BASEL

Public Schools/Private Enterprise
a TECHNOMIC®publication

Published in the Western Hemisphere by
Technomic Publishing Company, Inc.
851 New Holland Avenue, Box 3535
Lancaster, Pennsylvania 17604 U.S.A.

Distributed in the Rest of the World by
Technomic Publishing AG
Missionsstrasse 44
CH-4055 Basel, Switzerland

Printed in the United States of America
10 9 8 7 6 5 4 3 2 1

Main entry under title:
   Public Schools/Private Enterprise: What You Should Know and Do About Privatization

A Technomic Publishing Company book
Bibliography: p.
Includes index p. 169

Library of Congress Catalog Card No. 97-60458
ISBN No. 1-56676-535-8

CONTENTS

ACKNOWLEDGEMENTS

The seeds for this book were sown during an intensive experience in Michigan's Pinckney School District by one of the authors. Although, as described in the following chapters, the privatizing focus of that experience was unique, the demands for skill, inventiveness, and flexibility were not much different than those required daily of the superintendents of America's over 15,000 school districts. Often overlooked are the family members of the chief executive. They provide immense support during the crises that often beset their loved ones and must endure the effects that emotional stress and long hours at work impose on their loved ones. Our wives, Marilyn Flam and Gerry Keane, know only too well the demands of the superintendency on family life. We thank them for their continuing encouragement and patience, as well as substantive advice about the book's contents.

Many others contributed to making this book a reality. Dr. Clarence Jarboe wrote a dissertation about privatization at the University of Dayton, which gave substantive leads about the background literature on privatization. Brian Marcel, who served as Pinckney's Business Director, and whose wisdom, which far exceeds his age, helped immeasurably in dealing with the privatization discussions in Pinckney and added business acumen to the development of some concepts in the book as did Thomas Goulding, assistant superintendent for the West Bloomfield (MI) Public Schools. The knowledge and insights of Robert Boonin, an attorney with Butzel Long, provided invaluable help during the Pinckney experience and in the preparation of text dealing with legal issues. Loren Stone gave generous advice for the development of the appendix on contractual language. Dr. John McLaughlin, editor of *The Education Industry Report,* helped identify sources and resources. Attorney Timothy Gladney, former Pinckney School Board Trustee and practicing school attorney, reviewed selected sections of the book for accuracy. Gayle Roy provided special skill and assistance in developing many of the book's figures and illustrations.

Human history is shaped by the ebb and flow of fashion in ideas. Militarism turns to pacifism, prudishness is overthrown by permissiveness, immigrants arc acculturated in the melting pot then the salad bowl, formal dress gives way to casual garb. After a mind-set hits a peak of interest, a turnabout starts in the other direction, though perhaps not at the same level of commitment or fanaticism as before nor in the same time frame that gave rise to the original mental model.

The preferred role of government in the life of citizens is no less subject to these pendulum swings. The excesses of "bare knuckles" capitalism of the late nineteenth and early twentieth centuries in the United States eventually gave way to the "New Deal," marked by a conviction that only government could balance and control the needs of business and the welfare of citizens. The Russian empire gave way to Communism. The Soviet Bloc now moves back fitfully toward a market economy. America is currently engaged in a wholesale effort to "reinvent government" by making it smaller, less expensive, and less obtrusive. To a large extent the present American electorate seems to have tried government solutions, at least for the poor, and found them largely wanting. The market, many politicians assert, is the only effective cure for what ails us. It is the only vehicle, they argue, that will permit human freedom to flourish and invention and creativity to thrive.

It is in this phase of the history of ideas in America that privatization has become a topic of close scrutiny and sometimes impassioned debate. Assumptions about why certain services should be delegated to public providers are being reconsidered. Some would argue that a few services, for example golf course construction and management, a common government service in the twentieth century, ought not to be a government responsibility at all. The resources of all should not, it is maintained, be used to respond to the interests of few and the needs of none. Other services, and here education takes a high profile in the debate, may need the guarantee of public support and oversight but not the perceived drawbacks of public management. Public officials are urged to "steer, not row." Even President Clinton and Vice President Gore, members of the same party that virtually invented big government in America, moved toward this line of thinking through the National Performance Review, a 1993 study to find ways to make government "work better and cost less."

This book attempts no political or philosophical conclusions about whether privatization within or of public education is sound or unwise public policy, whether it is compelling theory likely to impact public education for decades or a temporary phenomenon likely to disappear. Privatization may prove to be both. There is reason and evidence to support the view that the increasing privatization of non-instructional functions may continue for a long time. The transfer of instructional responsibilities for individual schools or total districts to private companies has a much shorter and more volatile track record. As a consequence, future trends are much less predictable in this area.

Several conclusions are, however, certain. Interest in introducing market forces into all public services, including education, has not peaked. More and more states are looking at charter schools and voucher plans as potential stimuli to improved student achievement. A number of entrepreneurs have recognized the mood of the country and assessed the profits that might be made from a potential customer base of fifty million K–12 students, and the number of these companies is likely to grow. With this growth will come political pressure to open up the education "market" to business.

Therefore, it is quite likely that most, if not all, school districts will at least need to think through the possibilities of privatizing one or more functions. As more and more states move to achieving financial equity in education by increasing the state's role in funding schools, schools will experience less control over revenues and, equally likely, less revenue as prison construction and operation and devolved social welfare costs eat up a larger percentage of state budgets. Privatizing operation of expensive ancillary services within the education industry can also remove the onus of going to taxpayers directly to raise the funds necessary to support these services.

But privatizing services is hardly a simple solution to cost effectiveness or cost efficiency problems. Public employee salaries have increased dramatically in the last generation. While at one time public employees sacrificed income to gain employment security, it is the public's perception, and there is data to support it, that public employees now have both more income and more protection than comparable private sector workers. However, many public employees work in the political jurisdiction that employs them. They understandably do not want to give up either the income or security that it has taken them a long time to gain. Their family and friends do not want to see them hurt either. Parties on all sides of the issue can be expected to vote. As a result, the volatile elements are mixed. If a potential contract to privatize is put on the school board table for consideration, the flame is lit. The ensuing community conflagration can be awesome.

This book is written to help all concerned parties—school board members, administrators, parents, and other community residents—who choose to or who must endure the privatization debate. Hopefully, good information will provide protection against immolation for all sides. It is probably inevitable that every such discussion will cause at least a small fire in the community. If there is a fire, our goal is to control the flames with the smothering power of knowledge and practitioner experience.

This book is intended to provide a useful balance of scholarship and craft knowledge honed in the crucible of a real community debate about privatizing a local school district. Hopefully, readers, and leaders, will encounter the twin tools of theory and practice out of which enlightened action can flow. As two former practicing superintendents we have learned, sometimes the hard way, that a leader needs both.

SAMUEL FLAM
WILLIAM G. KEANE

CHAPTER 1

The Pinckney Experience: To Hell and Back

Although the student population of the Pinckney School District is approximately 3,900, it spans two Southeast Michigan counties. Pinckney is within driving distance to Ann Arbor, with many University of Michigan employees living in this bedroom community. It is also within driving distance to work sites of many Fortune 500 companies. Many residents of Pinckney are second- and third-generation farm families. Although dozens of new subdivisions have been under construction since the early 1990s, much recreational land is still available for further residential development.

Within the school district boundaries rests a tiny little crossroads whose notoriety far outstrips its importance, a town with the improbable name of Hell, Michigan. Although Hell is only a dot on the map, every TV weatherperson capitalizes on the name by adding it as a permitted blasphemy in the forecast. But Hell became symbolically more important to me as my assignment as the interim superintendent for the Pinckney School District turned from days into months. On one particularly stressful day, I drove to Hell to be able to report to my wife that on that day I had been to "Hell and back."

BEGINNING THE ASSIGNMENT

After nineteen years in the central office as deputy superintendent and superintendent of schools, interacting with the myriad issues which every superintendent confronts, be the assignment a large or small district, I arrogantly believed that there were going to be few surprises when I accepted the role of interim superintendent of the Pinckney School District. Was I wrong! After the unsuccessful attempt of some community members (and staff) to recall four of the seven board members, I answered the request of the Pinckney Board to serve as interim superintendent in two-week renewable increments. A short-term assignment was compatible with my schedule as an independent consultant. But the initial two weeks turned into a seven-month, fascinating, uncharted journey into the world of privatizing in public education.

The stage was set for my experiences as Pinckney's chief administrator during a most memorable meeting. On my third morning, just after learning the names of central office staff and finding the closest men's room, the board's president and secretary entered unannounced into my office. These gentlemen represented the board majority, five board members of seven. Four of them had been instrumental in the resignation of the previous superintendent. All supported serious consideration of privatizing the district's management. At this meeting it was revealed that they had invited Education Alternatives Incorporated (EAI) to make a presentation on privatizing the district. The public meeting at which this possibility would be discussed was scheduled for the following Monday.

These board members were urged to slow down the process. I reminded the president and secretary that they had just survived a divisive recall campaign. I argued that inviting EAI into the district without more notice to the public, without a clear statement of a reason for doing so, and without involvement of the functional leadership of the district would serve to exacerbate the polarization within the community, which was in desperate need of healing because of a recent unsuccessful election to recall the school board. After listening carefully, they excused themselves to call EAI. Upon their return to my office, they stated that it was too late. EAI's public relations' consultant had already placed an advertisement in the regional paper announcing the EAI presentation the following Monday. At the time, EAI's action was interpreted by some as an effort to wrest control of the activities and momentum from the board and superintendent. Reestablishing school district control over subsequent events became a significant focus of our efforts.

Since I had been involved in privatizing my prior district's food service operation, I naively thought I understood the dynamics with which I would be confronted. However, what I had not uncovered during my discovery process prior to agreeing to serve the Pinckney district was the board's interest in privatizing the entire management of the district, including the educational process. I knew that the board majority had already investigated contracting busing service and facilities management. Their commitment to privatizing had been one of two major causes for a recall of the four majority board members, a recall campaign that was spearheaded by some members of the local affiliate of the Michigan Education Association (MEA) and joined by some district administrators. The precipitating event for the recall, in so far as I could determine, seemed to be the dismissal of the superintendent. According to information later provided by central office staff, even the superintendent's dismissal was influenced by the board's focus on privatizing. One administrator related that during negotiations with a transportation vendor, the vendor told the board that the superintendent was interfering with the movement toward privatizing.

The day I was appointed as interim superintendent, a fifth board member resigned. She also had been involved in the unsuccessful effort to recall the board majority. The four-member board majority successfully grew to five when they appointed an ally for a six-month replacement term to take her place. As I discovered over my first few weeks, several of this board majority mistrusted almost the entire administrative team, especially since many central office staff had contributed to the recall campaign.

There were two lawsuits against the board when I began my tenure, one brought by the prior superintendent, and a second that resulted from the board's prior attempt to privatize the busing service. Over the succeeding months several more suits were filed by the MEA affiliate. These appeared to be an attempt to slow down the privatizing effort. In one case, a suit was filed against the board and the interim superintendent related to the interim's salary contained in the contract extension. Seemingly every possible effort was employed to use legal relief as an avenue to make more difficult the board's effort to privatize the district.

GATHERING CLOUDS

The first issue to be confronted in dealing with the privatization issue was how to reduce the negative impact of springing EAI's presentation on an unwary community. Although EAI had placed an insert in a regional newspaper, we had to give this event as wide an audience as possible. Fortunately, the school district's cable channel proved to be a good communication tool. Ultimately, communicating with a wide audience turned into one of the largest challenges that the district faced.

Monday came and EAI representatives made their presentation. They asserted that they were willing to put several million dollars into the district, if the district would turn over the total operation (including the management of the budget and the educational program) to the private companies they had brought together in a consortium they called the "Alliance For Schools That Work" (KPMG Peat Marwick, National Bus Company, Johnson Controls, Computer Curriculum Corporation, and led by EAI). The presentation used videotapes and experts from the Alliance, one from each of the five companies. The main attraction of their proposal was the several million dollars that the Alliance would immediately invest to initiate the school improvement process. The prevailing response from the audience that night and throughout the many months of negotiations was "There is no free lunch; what's the catch?" The presentation had all the earmarks of a well-financed marketing effort. It was a professional presentation. But when analyzing the substance of the presentation, there was no statement of guaranteed results should the Alliance be given the opportunity to manage the entire school district.

At the conclusion of their presentation, the president of EAI asked for a "letter of commitment" that pledged the board and the Alliance to a due diligence process. Each was to collect data and to work toward agreeing to a contract over the following few months. A "letter of intent" was signed at a board meeting Thursday of the same week, and the controversy began.

DECIDING TO STAY

I felt like a babe in the woods those first few days. I struggled to get a focus on what it all meant. I didn't have clarity about whether I was for or against the board's goals. I wasn't sure whether or how I could impact the process for arriving at a carefully considered decision. I had no idea what process I should propose for conducting a study. I tried to step back from the tempest while, at the same time, being requested to respond to questions for which I had no answers, no manual, no personal experience, and no colleagues within reach who had endured a similar adventure. But I did have one luxury; I was an interim superintendent. I didn't need the job, so I could look upon events as a learning experience. And learn I did.

I had to decide quickly where I stood on this accelerating bullet train. I could bail out. I had a two-week contract, which was rolling over for a second two weeks. After all, I felt suckered into the position without being told about the pending movement toward privatizing the entire district. This was a very hot national issue. Did I want or need the tension that was sure to follow? Months later, at a presentation to a university graduate class of aspiring superintendents, I was asked the question, "Why didn't you just say good-bye?" Maybe I should have, but it turned out to be energizing, intellectually stimulating, and an unequaled challenge—but not one for which I had been prepared.

In order to decide whether or not to remain on the job as the board's CEO, I had to resolve where I personally stood on the privatizing issue. This had to get settled quickly. The high school principal asked me to address his staff in the days following the initial EAI presentation. This was a staff that felt betrayed by the board majority, which had been responsible for forcing out their respected previous superintendent and, to add insult to injury, was now considering turning over the district to a group of unknown entrepreneurs.

I approached the privatizing debate before the high school staff based on my view of myself as a professional educator. This led me to a set of guiding principles that operated as a benchmark for personal and professional actions and responses throughout my Pinckney tenure. As an educator, I had to be open to new ideas and the possibility that changing the system in some way might enhance the learning opportunities for students. And I view learning as change: changing attitudes, skills, and knowledge. Therefore, educators cannot be ideologues, opponents of new techniques or ideas that conflict with our current paradigms. Our role forces us to examine every idea for its merit, its value in improving educational results. New ideas, processes, or products should not be viewed as inherently good or bad. Further, as a professional I am required to make decisions that are for the greater good. Since every decision has advantages and disadvantages, all professionals are called on to make choices that may even be personally distasteful but must be made when their clients benefit. It seemed that the Pinckney staff understood and appreciated my position. I told them that I respected their right to investigate the facts of the board's initiative and to voice their concerns. My job would be to assure ample time for careful deliberations. Nevertheless, many skirmishes erupted around these rights as we moved forward in the debate.

INFLUENCING THE DECISION-MAKING PROCESS

Major challenges followed those first few weeks. It was not my role to decide the final outcome of the privatizing investigation. But the superintendent had a responsibility to influence the process in a way that would maximize a good decision that would be understood, even if not approved, by all significant groups. The attributes of the process that required thought and invention included the following:

- moving deliberately and not too hastily to a conclusion
- involving all major stakeholders in the community in the discovery process, but not allowing the process to be controlled by any of a number of existing and emerging powerful lobbies
- protecting the ongoing educational process during the stressful months of decision making
- encouraging full and free expression but not letting the emotion of the moment destroy reason
- encouraging conclusions derived from good data
- attempting to assure that any eventual contract with EAI or their partners was in the best possible interest of the children
- giving guidance to the formulation of the contract, if one was to be signed

KEEPING THE DISTRICT MOVING FORWARD

In addition to the privatization debate, the district faced three very important issues that would impact education in the Pinckney schools for many years: hiring the next superintendent of schools, conducting a millage campaign for much needed funds, and negotiating the next teachers' contract. Each of these issues was impacted significantly by the EAI initiative. These activities are always complicated; each requires well-executed strategies to be successful. But these undertakings were made immensely more complicated because of the objections to privatization, rational and emotional, which intruded upon the daily life of the school district.

Selecting the Superintendent

EAI wanted to select and employ the next superintendent should the Alliance be hired to manage the district, since, from their point of view, satisfactory implementation of any privatization effort is highly dependent on the commitment of the district administration to make it work. When their representatives discovered that Michigan law required that the superintendent be hired by the board, they shifted to trying to influence the superintendent selection process. However, it seemed a patent conflict-of-interest for EAI to be influential in selecting the superintendent who would then oversee and monitor their contract.

The company suggested that it would not be difficult for them to find a capable administrator to become the Pinckney superintendent, since they could offer a transfer within the company's organization if the Pinckney relationship were to be prematurely terminated. Since this guarantee of future employment gave the company significant leverage over the superintendent's decisions, provision had to be included in the superintendent's contract to make certain that the chickens were protected from the fox. Administration was successful in convincing the board to hire an outside consulting firm to assist the board in its executive search. Also, the board accepted the recommendation that a clause be inserted into the superintendent's contract that restricted him/her from working for a company that had privatized a district service for a period of two years after leaving the district.

Passing a Millage

The Pinckney School District community had voted against the prior five requests to raise the district's millage. This disdain for property taxes within the district was the board's argument for seeking privatization as an alternative means for funding that was desperately needed for improvements in operations and in acquiring educational technology. Under Michigan statute the district's property tax revenue was best protected by a millage renewal vote in June, five months, almost to the day, following the introduction of EAI to the district by the board majority. It was first necessary to get unanimous support for the millage from the board, the same board whose majority members won their seats by promising no new taxes. School staff are almost always supportive of a millage request. However, staff and many in the community anticipated that higher tax revenues would result in more profit for any company that received a contract. Strategies had to be developed that persuaded district staff and the community of the shortcomings of this logic. By involving administrators in planning for the devastating effects of the millage failure, especially if a contract with EAI was *not* signed, we were able to unlink the millage request from the privatizing effort, and the millage was approved.

Negotiating Contracts

Prior to the election of the board members who assumed control as a majority, labor peace had been a tradition of the district. But a palpable antagonism existed between the board majority and the unions by the time I was appointed. Even many of the building and district administrators were at odds with the board majority. Administrative contracts were up for renewal as was the teacher contract. EAI publicly maintained that a contract with them to manage the district would continue teachers and building level administrators as employees of the district. Central office clerical and administrative staff, teacher aides, and others were much less certain about their futures. This uncertainty added to the district's instability and diverted considerable energy away from providing Pinckney's quality education about which district staff openly expressed pride.

Gaining the board's understanding that an agreement to extend administrative contracts for two years would provide a degree of equilibrium so badly needed was a difficult task. Old wounds served to derail the central issue during discussions with the board. Ultimately, tensions and the need for stability surrounding the privatizing activity helped secure the board's commitment to a two-year extension of all administrative contracts. A silver lining had emerged.

But no silver lining appeared for teacher contract negotiations. It was rumored that the Michigan Education Association's (MEA) regional bargaining group, of which Pinckney's local MEA affiliate was a member, was more interested in using the negotiations process to manage the labor response to privatizing than they were in securing a contract for their membership. An indication of this reaction to privatizing was the sudden and unscheduled change in local union leadership to a president who used a more strident voice immediately following the announcement that EAI was interested in their school district. The MEA organized regional information meetings with teachers and affiliated staff. But after these meetings the emotional pitch of the dialogue with MEA seemed to escalate. Administrators received reports from these meetings that MEA representatives were telling their local membership that they must hold their ground, that the future of their colleagues was at stake in Pinckney's move toward privatization.

A BIGGER ISSUE

Events of each passing day proved that the forces at work in the Pinckney School District were beyond the control of the major players in this drama: the Pinckney Board, students, community, and staff. It was as if a huge conflagration among the pro and con privatization giants was taking place all around us. Once this became apparent we tried to reach out directly to the leadership of the state teachers association, which wielded considerable influence over the Pinckney teacher association and other district employee groups, to see if the rancor could be reduced. No accommodation proved possible.

MEA was against privatizing, period! When we appealed for MEA assistance in helping to heal the community rift that they seemed to be creating, Pinckney was promised MEA staff assistance only if and when EAI was dropped from consideration by the board. However, MEA offered as an alternative to privatizing their Pioneer School program, which they claimed would improve learning. There were at the time several school districts throughout the state that had implemented this site based decision-making program at a school. This offer gave the opening to set up negotiations with MEA and Pinckney teacher leadership to achieve a master agreement for teachers. As part of these discussions, Pinckney administrators, board members, MEA leadership, and other Pinckney union representatives explored a substitute plan to provide the resources that would make an agreement with the Alliance unnecessary.

After a few successful negotiating sessions, MEA implemented a strategy that infuriated participating board and administrative staff. An attorney who worked for MEA was appointed by them to speak on behalf of the Pinckney teachers in the local negotiations. In his initial comments to the group he downplayed the progress that the group had made and the sincerity of the board members, thereby undermining any potential for the MEA alternative to succeed. When we complained to the MEA office, officials there refused to recognize the effect this new negotiations leader would have. Subsequently, teacher negotiations continued through the summer and into the winter without a contract being reached in time for the beginning of the new school year.

It was impossible to determine the truth of a rumor that the MEA was stalling all issues to enable the election of a more pro-MEA board slate. Many months later a well-financed campaign was effective in unseating board majority incumbents and in the unseating of anti-privatization candidates. However, this change in board composition did not quickly result in a new teacher contract.

DIVIDING THE PIE

Curiosity from outside the district, especially media interest, rivaled the interest of Pinckney School District residents. Days, bleeding into weeks, were spent in responding to media inquiries from all over the country. Newspapers, TV stations, syndicated media, and political groups in multiple numbers each wanted the attention of the superintendent, board members, teachers, and students. The board president was heavily involved in responding to the media's request for personal interviews.

Extreme right-wing advocates, who often came from other states, picketed the high school so as to benefit from the media spotlight. Managing the demand for film footage, interviews, and phone responses required the creation of new approaches. A board meeting was never held without the media present, which resulted in grandstanding by all sides. The board meeting at which the interim superintendent was hired had had about twenty people in the audience. Every meeting thereafter had no fewer than 400 sitting in the audience for the twice a month board meetings, which were permanently moved to the high school cafeteria and often lasted until 1 and 2 A.M. Many of those in the audience wanted to address the board over and over, restating their position. Emotions ran very high at every Pinckney School Board meeting. Crowd control techniques became an even higher priority after a superintendent in the adjacent school district was shot and killed by a mentally deranged teacher.

MANAGING THE PROCESS

Although I had been lobbying in private to the contrary, the board majority introduced a motion that discussions regarding the EAI relationship be delegated to a board subcommittee. I objected by pointing out that gaining community support for the eventual outcome was critical and that open discussions and wide participation were the keys to such support. As usual, there were over 500 attending the public meeting at which I made this statement and the board acquiesced by appointing a community committee to assist the board in conducting its "due diligence" review. I simultaneously established a superintendent's committee to gather questions to be addressed by the board's committee and ultimately the board. These questions, which numbered in the hundreds, eventually formed the basis of the contract negotiations with EAI.

In addition to keeping open the dialogue, the information gathering process helped the due diligence period grow from weeks into months. Concern over the possibility that the board wanted to railroad a contract with EAI diminished as meetings of these two committees continued.

PRIVATIZATION: GOOD OR BAD?

It is difficult to answer in one word the question I have been asked many times: should the Pinckney Board have signed a contract with the Alliance? I did not then nor do I now agree with the process the board majority used to introduce the Alliance to the community, nor did I agree with those board zealots who saw privatizing as the only solution to the district's financial problems. However, a contract with the Alliance could have been good for Pinckney students if it had included the terms that we sought. The many contract inclusions that we presented, and which to a large degree were acceptable to Alliance representatives, provided needed safeguards and many resources for the educational program. (See the appendixes for a listing of some of the contract issues and provisions that a district might consider in writing a contract with a private company for service.) Would the same contract have been good for some other district? Maybe not. I did come to realize one very important caveat: privatizing is neither inherently good nor bad—it is situational. It is the right or wrong decision based upon the district's specific circumstances and the company's final offer. But privatizing district services should be one of the alternatives available in maximizing the resources for learning.

SUMMARY

It is the experiences described in this chapter that suggested the need for this publication. After completing the assignment, it became apparent that the lessons learned about the complexity of moving to contracting with an outside company were relevant beyond this singular experience. Many times during my Pinckney tenure, guidance was sought in the literature and from colleagues, but little practical assistance was available. Therefore, this publication has been designed to provide practical information to guide those who may grapple with the policy and procedural issues related to privatizing one or more school district functions.

The authors are convinced that there is a growing and powerful momentum toward privatizing in the education marketplace. It is hoped that the contents of this book will be of help in preventing or at least anticipating the mistakes that have too often been experienced "under fire."

CHAPTER 2

Privatization: Premises and Precedents

The superintendent was surprised by the board member who called to request that a resolution be placed on the next board meeting agenda to initiate an investigation of privatizing the district's custodial services. The superintendent immediately informed the custodial union of the board member's request.

Three hours later the local's president, vice president, and American Federation of School, County and Municipal Employees (AFSCME) regional president sat nervously at the superintendent's conference table. Their reaction to the proposed agenda item was hostile. The AFSCME president threatened the district with pickets at the next board meeting. He also claimed the proposed study to be illegal as long as the existing labor agreement, which had another seventeen months to run, was still in effect. He implied that the resources of AFSCME would be behind the district's local and that injunctive relief would be sought to stop the board from any such discussions. At the next meeting picketers, many of whom appeared to be strangers, carried signs protesting the study as an attempt to "bust the union." Five days later the board attorney was in court arguing against the custodial union's request for injunctive relief.

PRIVATIZING: A PEOPLE PROBLEM

The school practitioner hoping to improve school services for students and/or patrons by hiring a private company to provide a function previously delivered by district employees or the citizen reading about the resulting school district controversy flowing from this decision may

13

initially be hard-pressed to understand why this issue is so volatile. The answer is simple. Carrying out such a shift is a people problem. It can involve the minds, hearts, and pocketbooks, often all three, of those affected by a decision to change a past practice. Practically every such decision is seen by chief school administrators as a ticking box with a "don't touch" sign on it.

Many of the events described in the first chapter are not atypical in school districts attempting to privatize a service, especially those doing so for the first time. The Pinckney situation was exacerbated by the fact that the board's intended action would impact virtually every employee in the district. Employee attempts to oppose this change are under-standable. At least some of the board's motivation, to use scarce dollars more effectively for instruction, are rational. Both sides are acting out of beliefs and value systems that can hardly be faulted. However, as so often happens in human events, when fundamental interests are at stake on both sides of a conflict, actions can get out of hand. Emotion can overcome reason. Long-term damage to the effectiveness of a school district is often the result.

More and more efforts are being made to reinvent the present organization of public education in America. Some of these initiatives are fundamental attacks on the concept of public schools for all, paid for by all. California's unsuccessful referendum in 1993, which would have created a voucher program to allow public dollars to flow to any public or private school, was the most dramatic symbol of efforts to change the traditional system of public education. At least twenty-five states and the District of Columbia at this writing have charter school options, public schools established and run outside the formal school governance system. Milwaukee (Wisconsin), Cleveland (Ohio), and other jurisdictions are attempting to explore on a small scale the use of public dollars in private education settings.

It is within a climate of general citizen dissatisfaction with public education and a strong politically conservative movement among the electorate that the issue of "privatization" has become a matter of public debate. This publication will have two goals: to explain the recent growth of interest in privatization and to help readers focus on the substantive issues of running schools as professionally as possible without engaging in philosophical/political debates about an abstract concept. A pragmatic approach to the issue permits a careful analysis of real options for improving school effectiveness and efficiency.

PRIVATIZATION: WHAT IS IT?

As Savas (1987) has pointed out, the term *privatization* entered the dictionary only in very recent times. He could find no entry for the word before 1983 (p. 3). More importantly he notes that "the very word 'privatization' unfortunately summons forth images from a deep reservoir and causes misunderstanding, premature polarization, and shrill arguments that are beside the point more often than not" (p. 277). Therefore, though it is important to have a shared meaning for a word that has grown common in public discourse, it is the activities that the word denotes which are of significance to those interested in public education, not the penumbra of feelings and emotions that are generated when the word itself is discussed.

At a literal level the term refers to the process of turning over to private companies programs, services, and sometimes properties previously operated and/or owned by a government agency. This may be done in whole or in part. However, it may well be argued that contracting out a function or service to a private company while maintaining in the hands of the public governing body ultimate responsibility for the quality and efficiency of the results does not really constitute privatizing in a literal sense. The options for privatizing will be discussed later.

HISTORY OF PRIVATIZATION

An International Perspective

There are several reasons for the growing popularity of privatization. The concept represents a worldwide political movement that has made its mark on almost all countries. Its rise internationally can be attributed, among other factors, to the downfall of Marxism as a viable political philosophy. Country after country in the Eastern Bloc of nations, following the lead of the Soviet Union, has largely rejected the idea that government ownership of all means of production can lead to prosperity. Many nations in Africa and South America have recently embraced, at least at the theoretical level, a new commitment both to capitalism and democracy. The effects of this global sea change in thinking have been profound. Not only were Marxist countries fundamentally impacted by this reversal in economic thinking; many Western countries, most especially England, voted out dominant political parties committed to Socialism and began a rapid movement toward privatizing. Not only were the industries that had been in private hands prior to Socialist governance privatized; many functions that had been traditionally provided by government agencies were also placed in the hands of private companies. English Prime Minister Margaret Thatcher's efforts to privatize government services were so great that one writer described the results of her government's efforts as "the largest transfer of power and property since the dissolution of the monasteries under Henry V" (Pirie, 1988, p. 4).

The American Experience

The political transformations leading toward privatization in other countries had an impact even in America, always a bastion of capitalism. Ronald Reagan was elected president of the United States in 1980 on a platform committed to downsizing government, both by reducing the taxes that support government services and by sloughing off to the private sector programs, services, and even properties owned by the government. Though this initiative was driven by the same political philosophy that was guiding English Prime Minister Margaret Thatcher in her major efforts to redefine and minimalize the role of government, other factors were also involved, some theoretical, some attributable to indigenous political factors.

The slowly eroding economic condition of the American middle class led to a disaffection with government among many. Some scapegoating was involved, including blaming the government for what was seen by some as giving unfair advantages and preferences to minorities in getting jobs and securing entry to colleges, universities, and professional schools. The strapped middle class also saw themselves taxed by government to provide what were seen as generous support payments to "lazy" welfare clients and cheats who were using the system to avoid work. Government efforts to increase control over weapons ownership, limit uses of private property, reduce dangerous health practices such as smoking, and carry out other forms of governmental regulation led to a political climate that stressed reducing the role of government (Florestano, 1985).

Other, less personal, arguments for reducing the role of government have been articulated. The existence of a global marketplace and world-wide competition requires less government regulation so that private businesses can respond quickly to the demands of the enlarged market-place. The very existence of this worldwide market provides protection against monopolistic practices that were previously the responsibility of government. The President's Commission on Privatization established by Ronald Reagan in 1983 also argued that governments are performing services that could easily be provided by the private sector at less cost since governments are monopolies and behave just like monopolies in the private sector, running inefficiently and impervious to the market-place.

HOW AND WHY DID GOVERNMENT GROW?

Americans have always imagined themselves as rugged individualists. Song, story, and visual art have always reflected the favorite American stereotype: the independent, strong, self-reliant citizen—the tamer of the frontier, the creative entrepreneur, the fearless warrior fighting for freedom at home and abroad, whether the enemy be Indians or Nazis. How then did government grow so big and take on so many responsibilities?

The Impact of Progressivism

Like any complex question there are no simple answers. The Commission on Privatization looked at the historical antecedents of big government and traced a good deal of the blame to the Progressive Movement of the late nineteenth and early twentieth centuries. Leaders of this movement were distressed by the negative social consequences of unfettered capitalism—poverty, sickness, crime—especially among citizens who were losing the competitive struggle for economic security. Proponents of Progressivism traced many of the failures of government to the incestuous commingling of politics, money, and bureaucratic power. The solution was to "professionalize" government service through a civil service system that would separate policy making and administration and also protect administrators from arbitrary dismissals by elected officials. Politics would deal with issues of value and other subjective questions not suitable to scientific resolution. Government workers would bring objective expertise to the resolution of public questions.

Therefore, the size and responsibility of government grew as efforts to manage market forces to socially desirable ends and provide services to the needy became public priorities. It is out of this Progressive tradition that a logical fallacy developed, which impacts the privatization debate today; that is, the notion that government workers are motivated to serve the public professionally and selflessly while private industry is motivated only by a desire to make a profit. This line of reasoning forces the conclusion that any program that serves the public should be provided by public workers. (This conclusion begs the question as to what services should rightly be described as the exclusive province of government.) Privatization thus becomes an emotionally laden issue not only because the economic well-being of government workers is involved but also because time has reinforced a stereotype that is clearly open to challenge.

The Depression Era

The enthusiasm for government as a provider of services may be said to have reached a fever pitch by the 1920s. It took a United States Supreme Court decision in 1925 (*Pierce v. Society of Sisters*) to overturn an Oregon law that required that all children be educated in the public schools and that prohibited private schools as an alternative. The stock market crash of 1929 and the subsequent economic depression gave rise to a growth in government services that was truly historic in its size and in the variety of tasks that became the responsibility of government for the first time. Most importantly the government became the employer of last resort; e.g., the Works Progress Administration (WPA) and the Civilian Conservation Corps (CCC). The addition of these responsibilities to government was due not so much to a Progressive Era idealism about the professionalism of government as to a factor of economic necessity. There simply were insufficient jobs available in the private sector to keep many families from starving.

After World War II

World War II gave the government a different vehicle for employing large numbers of citizens as millions of people were drafted into the military services over almost five years. The end of the war gave rise to still another role for supporting workers during the period of the late 1940s and 1950s: the G.I. bill, which provided family support as well as tuition for the hundreds of thousands of former military personnel who returned to school after their service obligation was completed. The War on Poverty initiated by the presidential administration of Lyndon B. Johnson witnessed the creation of a whole host of new government bureaus and services in an attempt to provide needed education and social services to the nation's poor.

Public Education: 1945–1970

While all this was going on, the nation's youth population was exploding as returning veterans were starting families after a long hiatus overseas. Suburbia grew exponentially, thereby leading to the almost overnight growth of new communities as former farm lands became subdivisions. New communities meant new roads to be maintained, refuse to be collected, recreational programs to be provided. All of these services required employees to provide them.

A paradoxical phenomenon was impacting school districts at this same time: the pupil population was growing and the number of school districts in the country was declining rapidly, from approximately 33,000 around 1945 to about 17,000 ten years later (Carlson & Awkerman, 1991). The argument for district consolidations was the opportunity to provide more services at a higher level of quality and efficiency than was possible in very small school districts. Therefore, the desire to provide better services meant the need to create more positions in areas such as student food service, pupil transportation, buildings and grounds maintenance, and others. With all the other examples of government employment as a natural phenomenon throughout society, it is hardly remarkable that school districts endeavored to hire their own employees to provide services, especially since the wages of government workers in this period trailed those of employees in the private sector. In addition, the opportunity to provide employment for local citizens meant that tax dollars stayed in the community and residents had an opportunity to gain what was seen as secure employment at a convenient location. Very often these newly employed residents had children attending school in the district so the economic needs of these taxpayers as well as their interest in assisting in the important task of educating their children could be fulfilled at once.

In general, private companies were not beating on the doors of municipalities and school districts to serve as contractors for services for many reasons:

- The U.S. economy had explosive growth after World War II. Returning veterans needed homes, cars, furniture, and other consumer goods, a situation that created jobs for almost everyone and therefore a growing national prosperity. There were plenty of opportunities in the private sector for private companies, which were themselves in a growing mode and incapable of taking on an inexhaustible number of clients/customers.
- A private company working within the rules, regulations, and reporting requirements imposed on governments also faced special problems, both political and economic, when attempting to do business in the public sector:
  (1) Bureaucratic rules, regulations, and reports were an added cost burden.
  (2) Any customer dissatisfaction could become a major public relations embarrassment including discussion before the governing body and news media accounts of citizen concerns.
  (3) In general, government dollars were limited so standards for service were low; therefore, the opportunity to maximize profit by providing "higher end" goods/services did not exist. As a result, governments became the employer of large numbers of citizens almost by default.

Political scientists who have studied public policy issues going back to the 1950s, long before any debate about privatization heated up, clearly demonstrated that government bureaus and government workers are subjected to the same human strengths and foibles as are corporations and workers in the private sector. Government workers "lobby" for their own economic interests just as private workers. For example, most government workers have the same or similar collective bargaining rights as workers in the private sector. Government bureaucracies also "lobby" for more functions and most especially for more budget. Most administrators of government services have the responsibility of their position, and therefore their salary level, determined by the amount of budget they administer. If the budget grows, so does the administrator's compensation.

But citizens lobby for the growth of government also. Traditionally government services have been seen as "free" because of the loose coupling in the minds of most individuals between the tax rate all pay and the "free" services delivered. The more services that government could be enticed to provide, the less the individual's responsibility to pay personally to get the same service.

Inevitably, at a time when the political pressures existed only to add services and grow budgets, questions of efficiency were hardly ever raised. Though the taxpayer was chagrined by the effect of this dynamic on his/her tax bill, the taxpayer was often hard-pressed to be sure that his/her rebellion against the general tax rate might not eliminate a favored service.

DOWNSIZING GOVERNMENT: THE INTEREST GROWS AND SPREADS

A very sharp turn in public thinking has taken place in recent years. All elected and appointed officials have felt the sharp claw of public opinion. Certainly the economic vise that has been closing on the middle class is contributing to this national mood. When most families see the need to have two wage earners to provide the same standard of living, not a very luxurious one at that, provided by one breadwinner a generation ago, the "party is over" for government. Issues related to the perceived unfairness of government policy and the obtrusiveness of government agencies helped to heat up the national dissatisfaction.

The cost of government is no longer transparent either. Savas (1987) has noted that "in about 50 years (1930–1983) government expenditures have grown a hundredfold, from an eighth to more than a third of the gross national product" (p. 14). In the period between 1948 and 1983 private sector employment grew at a compound annual rate of 1.8% while the government work force grew at 2.8% (p. 16). Considering the taxes required to support this rising work force and the services they provide, the increasing size of social security deductions from the biweekly check, and the growing need to co-pay higher percentages of employee fringe benefits, especially health insurance, the reasons for the public rage at the cost of government become easily understandable.

The universal distaste for taxes has impacted the thinking of appointed as well as government officials. (Some say a broken promise by George Bush not to increase taxes cost him a presidential election three years after his decision to support a tax increase.) Though costs of providing services continue to rise, especially personnel costs, the opportunity to acquire offsetting tax revenues has shrunk rapidly. Administrators and governing boards see privatizing as an opportunity both to maintain a service to the public without bearing the consequences of continually declining quality of that service or to suffer the wrath of citizens who believe that someone else's services should be cut, not theirs. Also, by taking this step they may move more comfortably into the general ideological pressure to downsize government (Lipset & Schneider, 1983).

PRIVATIZATION: THE CURRENT DEBATE

Tracing the antecedents of today's privatization debate is not easy. The federal government has been contracting out services and selling assets ever since the early years of the Republic, when it contracted out postal operations and sold public lands (Starn, 1991). The first modern initiative for privatization at the federal level is usually identified as Office of Management and Budget circular A76, first issued by the Bureau of the Budget in 1966, though its origins have been traced back to the Eisenhower administration in the 1950s. It generally required the federal government "to use commercial services if such an approach is less expensive than public production of these services by more than 10%" (Pack, 1991, p. 296).

Perhaps the most potent tools used by politicians at the national and state level to bring about privatization have been tax reductions and deregulation. Deregulation of the trucking and airline industries immediately eliminated the need for bureaucratic structures to monitor those industries. Without tax revenues governments are forced to choose between maintaining services at increasingly poor levels of quality or eliminating services, always a controversial decision. Especially at the local and state levels, where there has been evidence of the likelihood of providing services at a lower cost through privatization, this approach has become an increasingly more popular option for the delivery of services. The privatization of prisons would have been unthinkable a generation ago. Now that support for the criminal justice system is becoming one of the fastest growing functions within state budgets, more and more states are experimenting with privatizing prisons.

However, local and state governments have a long history of employing private companies to carry out tasks, especially those that required personnel with specialized skills or expensive equipment and that were performed infrequently. It made no sense to employ narrowly trained staff or buy exotic equipment to build a bridge, a highway, or a tunnel since such projects came along quite sporadically (Doyle, 1994). In the mid-1960s, as government expanded its role of providing assistance to the poor, the elderly, "at risk" children and youth, and other targeted populations, federal, state, and local government agencies were required to seek the assistance of private companies to provide selected services, since audiences for these services might be very small in any one location. It would clearly be foolish to create an infrastructure to serve small numbers of clients who might be located at geographically separated sites.

As a result both public (non-profit) and private agencies were called on to provide such services as "meals on wheels" to shut-ins or transportation for the elderly and the poor, who needed to get to sites for education programs or job training. Thus society has gradually drifted into a "rich mosaic of private-public interaction . . . (achieved) in part by differentiating the policy, financing, ownership, operation, and management aspects of public services" (Atherton and Windsor, 1987, p. 82).

HOW CAN GOVERNMENTS PRIVATIZE?

Before looking at ways to privatize government functions it is necessary to return to a definition of privatization. In a narrow sense, privatization means the devolution to private enterprise the operation of services previously provided by a government agency. This transfer refers not only to the delivery of the function or service but the policy-making structure that guides the ends and means of providing the function/service. It also means that the private provider is singularly accountable for quality and cost. Perhaps the only techniques of privatization that bring about this result are those in which a service is deregulated or a function is sloughed off by government. Both are still relatively rare forms of privatization.

In a broader sense the term *privatization* has been used "to describe the full range of options by which we may increase private participation in the provision of services" (Atherton and Windsor 1987, p. 82). The more common forms of privatization usually involve some form of contracting. School officials need to keep this distinction regarding the meaning of privatization in mind when considering the possibility of contracting out a service previously provided by government employees. When a service is contracted, the governmental body still maintains responsibility for the kind and quality of service. It defines its desires through the specifications it draws for services when seeking bids from private providers. Some have even argued that privatization in these forms "can be more responsive to public policy than governmental agencies for it is easier to influence the behavior of a private organization than the behavior of a public agency" (Savas, 1987, p. 105).

By definition a contract is for a fixed period of time. The pressure is on the contractor to satisfy the client. If the contractor provides unsatisfactory service, another vendor can usually be quickly found to pick up the contract. (If this situation isn't true, then the school district might be better served by not privatizing. More about that later.) It can also be argued that it is much harder to improve a service provided by the district's employees, who are possibly unionized and therefore may be hard to influence, or who almost certainly are predominantly residents of the district and whose behaviors may be difficult to change for political reasons.

RANGE OF OPTIONS FOR PRIVATIZING

From a technical point of view privatization usually takes one of the following forms when government agencies seek to reduce costs or increase quality. Each of these strategies has many permutations and combinations:

- sale of public properties, in whole or part
- contracting out a function or service (e.g., refuse collection)
- load shedding (e.g., turning over the operation of a public facility like a golf course to a private company. This can differ from the usual forms of contracting in that the private company operates semi-independently of the governmental body even in relation to policy issues. The government usually gets a defined portion of profits if there are any.)
- user charges (Government continues operations but charges for use of the facility or function; for example, one school district in Michigan charges anyone who visits their innovative school, including teachers and administrators, $25 for the visit.)

- withdrawal from providing a function (Privatization may be the result but it is not the primary goal of the government agency.)

PRIVATIZING IN PUBLIC EDUCATION: THE CURRENT STATUS

It is not the purpose of this book to discuss the full scope of involvement by the private sector in public education. There has always been a portion of K–12 education that has been provided by non-public, not-for-profit agencies. In the nineteenth century public education was "a three sector industry: schools for profit as well as denominational schools served large sections of the population" (Lieberman, 1993, p. 14). Today, schools sponsored by the various major religions make up a significant portion of this cohort of schools. There is also a very small but growing number of independent for-profit schools opening around the country (Miller, 1995). Both of these types of schools are important within the nation's education delivery system but not within the focus of this publication, which looks at the effects of privatization on public education.

Noncontracting Forms of Privatization

The vast majority of privatization initiatives within education currently consist of some form of contracting. Therefore, major attention in this work will be paid to contracting issues, whether for support services such as transportation, food service, building and grounds maintenance and operations; or for instructional services, which may be for the full educational program in one or more schools or for some slice of the educational program, such as foreign language, remedial education, or one or more of the arts.

However, the other forms of privatization listed above have had at least a small impact on public education. Some of the more common forms of privatization are as follows:

Sale of Properties

The student population explosion of the 1950s and 1960s required a burst of school construction unique in the country's history. The rapid drop in student enrollments in the 1970s left many school districts with empty buildings unlikely to be filled for a very long time, if ever. A number of these school buildings were sold to private interests for such uses as senior citizen housing, office buildings, television studios, and many other purposes. Districts on the outer fringes of suburbia have sold off vacant properties to private interests when it became clear that population movements would not require these properties for the building of schools.

Load Shedding

When contracting is not included under this term, this process is a relatively rare phenomenon in education. A few school districts, lacking the technology to provide state-of-the-art technology resources for adult education and training, have turned over their facilities to a private company that designs and delivers the adult training largely independent of the school board's policy-making authority. The district receives a percentage of the profits earned by the company.

User Charges

Schools have always had some manifestation of user charges. Until beyond mid-century school districts traditionally charged a textbook usage fee until courts found this practice unconstitutional. Student fees to attend sports, music, and other school events can be conceived as a form of user charges. Perhaps of more concern to some supporters of the concept of free public education has been the rapid growth of "pay for play" fees. If students desire to participate in competitive sports sponsored by the school, they or their families must pay a fee established to cover the costs of coaches, team transportation, uniform cleaning and replacement, and other program costs.

Withdrawal

This is not an uncommon process, especially in those school districts that have been financially challenged. Districts have dropped interscholastic sports and classes in art, music, and sometimes physical education with some regularity. The dropping of any service by a governmental body is not usually designed primarily as a privatizing effort. Privatizing is sometimes the result. Governments often hope it is the result and are especially willing to try this cost reduction strategy when they know or expect that a private vendor is waiting to pick up a program or service.

When sports programs are reduced, municipal programs are occasionally initiated or expanded. This, of course, is not really privatization. It is more likely that parents and citizens will step in to attempt to raise money privately in order to keep the program going—a difficult chore. This strategy seldom makes the angry public go away. Pay for play is the usual result if school funds are not available to support athletics.

Vouchers

Vouchers, instruments that guarantee payment of public funds for private school tuition, are a form of privatization somewhat particular to public education. They have a long and sometimes controversial history. After World War II former military personnel were permitted to attend any approved education or training institution of their choice, including those with religious sponsorship. Though the constitutionality of this procedure was defended on the basis that adults were capable of dealing with separation of church and state issues on their own, it has often been cited as a precedent for more recent attempts to utilize vouchers in K–12 education. A small K–12 voucher experiment was conducted in Alum Rock, California, in the 1960s, but the vouchers were limited to use in public schools.

Only recently have some experiments with vouchers supported by public funds been implemented on a limited basis. Milwaukee, Wisconsin, and Cleveland, Ohio, are two of the jurisdictions where families of students living in the inner city have been given the option of using the voucher at a privately sponsored school. The constitutionality of such programs has been challenged and is under review. If a case is appealed to the U.S. Supreme Court and the Court finds voucher programs constitutional, at least for non-sectarian schools, the scope and size of privatization efforts could increase rapidly. State authorization for income tax deductions for private school tuition could bring about the same result.

CONTRACTING AS A FORM OF PRIVATIZATION

By far the most common and perhaps longest enduring form of

privatization in public education is contracting. School districts have been contracting for transportation services for many years, especially in rapidly growing districts, which were hard-pressed to build the infrastructure necessary to support fleets that were burgeoning. In these and other situations, school districts contracted out part of the busing service, at least until the district could afford to build or acquire facilities to properly maintain a large number of buses. In recent years, as noted previously, contracting has expanded to other school district support functions. This form of privatization is so important and increasing so rapidly that the next chapter will be devoted exclusively to this subject.

Public/Private Partnerships

It is not the intention of this book to argue for or against privatization in any of its forms. It does seem appropriate, however, to suggest that all responsible school officials should consider how a public/private partnership might improve service to students and school district taxpayers; that is, allowing private entities to deliver functions that will remain under public control. It is obvious that the personal impacts on district staff affected by a shift to a private provider are important. This issue will be addressed later. It is, however, good logic and good policy to first decide *what* should be done, then consider *how* it should be done.

As Edward Savas (1987) has noted, today's challenge is "to achieve a better division of responsibilities and functions between government and the private sector in order to take advantage of the strengths of each and overcome the limitations of the other. The resulting partnership can best satisfy the wants and needs of the people in a manner consistent with the fundamental beliefs and values of a democratic society" (p. 291).

As one superintendent from Oregon noted: "We aren't necessarily trained, nor are we better than anyone else, at busing kids, providing food service, maintenance and custodial" (*New York Times,* January 31, 1996).

Nor should it be assumed that contracting out a service, especially a troublesome or cost inefficient one, will guarantee to solve the district's problems. There is no simple policy, no sure process to make contracting work. Lots of school districts have tried contracting and some of them have been hurt badly, sometimes in a court of law, sometimes in the court of public opinion. Others have benefited greatly. Knowing how and when to contract, the type of information this book attempts to provide, can be the critical variable in determining the result the district achieves.

Perhaps more importantly a school district cannot and should not allow economic issues to become the only point of concern in deciding whether to contract a service, a practice that may characterize much of the rest of American society at the midpoint of the 1990s. Most government services do not lend themselves to easy productivity improvements, no matter what vendors may suggest through their advertising. Government services generally suffer from what one economist has called "cost disease," a necessary and inevitable labor intensiveness. Ill-conceived efforts to "increase productivity" by contracting may lead to anger, resentment, and political retribution against school district policymakers and administrators and result in far larger and more numerous problems than were addressed in the privatizing initiative.

Likewise "making the values of commerce emperors of our souls," said Lord Dahrendorf, former director of the London School of Economics, "leads to the destruction of public spaces and the decline of services that go with them, the weakening of health systems and public education, transportation, and safety" (Lewis, 1995). Hopefully succeeding chapters can facilitate privatization initiatives that will be judged and managed by economic and human values simultaneously.

SUMMARY

The perceived role of government in the mind of citizens is subject to the same ebb and flow that impacts other forms of societal thinking and behavior. At one time many people came to the United States to escape an oppressive and omnipresent government and so they wanted as little government as possible. As the country grew it was necessary for the government to take on more responsibilities because an increasing population needed more public services. Also, unfettered individualism and unregulated business practices gave rise to abuses that required government intervention to protect the health and safety of the population. Almost inevitably, several decades of experiencing the rising cost of increased government services and the larger tax burden needed to support a larger government have led to a shift in public opinion regarding the role of government in human affairs.

The American public now seems to be indicating that it wants to continue most of the services and benefits it has but at a much lower cost and with a less intrusive government presence. This shift in public thinking has required government agencies to reexamine which services are necessarily provided by government and, even if a service is deemed appropriate to remain under public control, whether government workers are necessarily the ones to carry out the required functions. The term *privatization* sums up a trend, an international as well as national phenomenon, to turn over functions from government to the private sector and to contract with private entities to deliver services deemed appropriate for public control.

CHAPTER 3

Contracting as a Form of Privatization

In an attempt to save money, the financially strapped district had contracted out its food service operation. Though most district employees had been reemployed by the contracting food service company, they were hired at lower rates and lost their fringe benefits. Virtually every one of these employees was a resident of the school district, one composed of a majority of minorities. This change had a significant economic impact on many families.

Not long after the private vendor took over, the press received a call to attend the school board meeting. The new food service program would be discussed. "The hot dogs are green. They're green every day. I'm not having my kids risk their life and health eating green hot dogs," shouted one parent.

The story made the front page of the community's daily newspaper. Parents were frightened. They more frequently questioned their children about the food they ate each day in the cafeteria than they inquired about classroom learning. More and more parents began to come to the board meetings complaining that the food served in the cafeteria looked bad, smelled worse, tasted awful. The company was terminated at the end of the two-year contract. The school district was back in the cafeteria business.

INTRODUCTION

Fundamental debates are taking place today about the need for clear vision and a focused mission for public education. Society is again revisiting questions regarding what should be expected from its public schools. In recent years the voices of business leaders have been among the loudest in the discussion. Since the publication of *A Nation at Risk,* the quality of education has been portrayed as a matter of national economic survival. "World-class" standards, though not operationally defined by practically any persons or groups exhorting schools to meet these standards, have been suggested for practically all students in all basic subjects.

If schools are to meet these world-class standards, they will have to focus their resources on achieving these goals. Denis Doyle (1994), a prominent critic of the present state of public education, points out that schools must learn what Peter Drucker has argued to businesses in the private sector for a long time: optimize, don't maximize; that is, "do what you are good at and let others do what they are good at" (p. 31). He and many others have pointed out that public education has taken on responsibility for many of the social, economic, and medical problems of children and their families and, in some cases "used the former as an excuse not to fulfill the latter" (p. 31). School administrators and policymakers will find themselves more frequently required to explain whether it is the best use of their financial and human resources to directly employ staff to carry out all of the tasks necessary to operate a cost-effective, accountable school district.

Though the word *privatization* is now a buzz word that has emotionally laden connotations, the current debate about the role of private corporations operating within the public sector is really one of degree, not kind. It is only the parameters of a public/private partnership that are really currently under debate by all but the most extreme writers on the subject. Few would favor the abolition of public education, though admittedly several writers, credible or not, do come close to that suggestion (see Blumenfeld, 1981; High and Ellig, 1988; Lieberman, 1993).

There has always been involvement of private enterprise in public education. One of the most crucial tools of instruction, the textbook, is almost universally secured from a private vendor. Processed and unprocessed food is traditionally secured from a private source, then heated or cooked and served by district employees in the school cafeteria. There is no inherent reason why the line between public and private supplier needs to be drawn at the line of food production rather than food preparation. School districts don't build buses, but local staff usually drive and maintain them. An analogy can be developed for practically every item that has to be fabricated for use in the school, from boilers to bagels. The traditional line has been drawn for very obvious reasons: school districts could not cost efficiently produce durable products of almost any kind. The issue that is now being investigated throughout the public sector is whether service delivery technologies or the levels of expertise necessary to provide a function cost efficiently have changed sufficiently to suggest that a new line be drawn, one that leaves school personnel in charge only of those areas they know best, especially instruction.

CONTRACTING OUT SUPPORT SERVICES

Most professional personnel in schools, from the teacher in the classroom to the superintendent in the administrative office, have been trained in teaching and learning. Only in recent years have school business offices become more populated by individuals primarily trained in finance and accounting. Yet history has shown that it is the education trained personnel who are asked to manage or at least provide leadership and direction to support operations in transportation, food service, buildings and grounds maintenance, data processing, financial operations such as cash management, investing, occasional building construction, and many other non-learning related functions. Often the school bus fleet is larger than any other transportation system in the community. The school food service program is larger than any restaurant in town, sometimes serving more clients than all the community restaurants put together. These functions are "big business" in their own right.

On the whole, school officials have done an admirable job in managing these functions. For example, school bus transportation systems have an enviable safety record. Recently compiled statistics show that during the period 1976–1992 less than 0.4% of the 650,000 fatal traffic crashes were school bus related (U.S. Department of Transportation, 1992). School food service programs provide meals that are balanced nutritionally to large numbers of students in very short time periods. School building and grounds care is seldom noted to be below community standards. So why should contracting these services be an issue? Because each of the major support services provided by public schools is undergoing rapid changes in techniques and technology, changes that are negatively impacting a school district's ability to direct its financial resources to the main mission of the district—teaching and learning.

Cost Advantages of the Private Sector

Private businesses and corporations have two advantages in their pursuit of capital equipment that help to make them more effective and efficient than the public provider:

- They can depreciate the declining value of a capital asset.
- They can include the cost of purchasing new equipment in the price of the product or service they provide.

Schools do not have the opportunity to do either. As the cost of school bus operations increases—more costly fringe benefits for employees, more expensive operating costs (gasoline for buses, insurance), and so forth—the district is faced with putting larger proportions of its general fund, which may be declining because of voter induced tax limitations and other factors, into providing transportation for children. Consequently, less money can be allocated to learning technology and reduced class sizes, vital contributors to learning improvement.

Cost Disadvantages of Public Schools

In recent years states have grown less generous, because of their own fiscal problems, in supporting the purchase of school buses. School lunch programs have been suffering from similar cost escalation problems. Probably from the time that food service programs were initiated in public schools, school boards have been debating whether the lunch, and more recently, breakfast programs are a legitimate expense of the general fund budget or should be viewed as an ancillary service for which students should pay the full cost. Most districts have tried to keep the revenues and expenditures of the food service program in balance. They have almost always been unsuccessful. Their problems have been compounded in recent years by several factors:

- reductions in farm surplus commodities available through the federal government
- the growing taste for "fast food" on the part of American families and the resulting disinclination to purchase the "healthy" food offered by the school lunch program
- district "open lunch" policies, which permit older students to leave the building during the lunch period, often to eat at a local

McDonald's or a similar "fast food" restaurant. (In this sense the school lunch function has already been privatized.) Declining participation rates mean declining revenues, more general fund subsidies, and declining opportunities to spread the costs of new equipment among participants in the program.

The inability to take advantage of productivity improvements through new technology because of a lack of funds continues a vicious cycle. Inefficient equipment grows older and eventually requires expensive repairs. Personnel costs remain high because of the inability to acquire more cost efficient equipment. The district is forced to consume scarce resources for programs which, however meritorious in their own right, are not the main mission of the school district.

Paul Houston, executive director of the American Association of School Administrators (AASA), a national organization of school administrators with a focus on the school superintendency, and himself an author of a book defending the accomplishments of public education (1994), has recognized the long history of private corporations working in educational support services and the rationale for this to continue if not grow. He has noted:

> In the non-instructional areas, such as busing, lunchrooms, and custodial support, private sector management has been in school systems for a long time. However, these are the three areas that are most clearly aligned with private sector practices and can most easily yield efficiencies. There is nothing inherently educational in running a bus, serving a meal or sweeping a floor. These are all activities that have been done broadly in our society and certainly education has no special claim to being able to do these better. (p. 133)

CONTRACTING INSTRUCTIONAL SERVICES

Some of the issues that have contributed to privatizing support services in the past have now emerged in the relatively new initiatives to privatize instructional services, the one area in which educators feel that their expertise is unassailable.

There are many reasons for this growing interest:

- the general dissatisfaction with the results of public education, which is often articulated by business leaders and fostered by

press accounts of low achievement by American students in national and international tests of achievement
- impatience with the inability of public schools to acquire modern technologies in order to improve classroom instruction
- a growing perception that schools are attempting to alter the value systems that students learn at home
- a discontent arising from the belief that students are undisciplined and schools are unsafe
- an impression that public school teachers, especially those represented by labor unions, are overpaid and unmotivated to do better

Schneider and Houston (1993) and Berliner and Biddle (1995) have provided objective evidence that many of the premises upon which these views are based are inaccurate. Nevertheless, the public is looking for alternatives, and school officials, more often driven by shrinking financial resources, are also looking for options to present delivery systems. One option, private contracting, tends to fall into two categories: single function companies and comprehensive educational management corporations.

SINGLE FUNCTION CONTRACTING

Contracting for the provision of educational services is not an entirely new phenomenon. School districts have long had contracts with each other to provide shared services such as drug abuse counseling, alternative schools, and other programs not likely to be cost efficient in serving just one school district. School districts have shared bus repair facilities. States with intermediate units have encouraged the creation of contracts between multiple school districts and the intermediate unit for the economical provision of unusually costly programs (vocational education) or services to special populations (handicapped, disadvantaged, gifted and talented).

School districts have also written contracts with non-profit agencies to deliver targeted services. The emergence of new initiatives such as child care has led to agreements between agencies, sometimes co-funded by the United Way or a single social service agency, to supervise children in the early morning or provide after-school activities for "latchkey" children.

Education as a Niche Market

The employment of private companies to deliver instructional services has been a significant step in breaking the old paradigm of government's role in public education. Large and small initiatives are now beginning to smash the old "one size fits all" delivery system. When Chris Whipple, who initially invaded the public education market successfully with his Channel One classroom news service, announced that he would open a block of private schools that would provide better education than public schools for the same amount of money, he fired a shot across the bow of the education establishment that caught everyone's attention.

Quietly many more events were developing that were changing public schools into public/private partnerships for student instruction. In fact, one of the early initiatives of this kind came out of a site based decision-making agreement between the Dade County School District and the Dade County Federation of Teachers. In considering how to use building level budget dollars more effectively, teachers decided that having a district-employed foreign language specialist visit the building periodically was not producing desired results. They decided to drop the itinerant teacher and hire Berlitz Jr., a subsidiary of Berlitz International, which specializes in foreign language instruction for young people. Actually, Berlitz Jr. has been contracting to provide foreign language and English as a second language services to schools since 1987. In 1994–95 they operated in forty-one public schools and districts in ten states. Language Odyssey, based in Chicago, is another firm that specializes in second language instruction in Spanish and French at the elementary level ("Private Firms," 1995).

Are situations like this an indication of the failure of foreign language education in public schools? Not at all. Berlitz is a company with a special expertise in helping language learners move quickly to some degree of mastery. They have, for many years, helped business officials, government employees, college students, and others going overseas to acquire basic language proficiency. Consideration of a vendor with a documented history of success to provide this special skill makes sense to these districts.

There are also other benefits of contracting for foreign language instruction. It is often difficult to find competent language teachers, especially for those languages that may prepare young people to work in Japan, China, Russia, and other countries that may be the center of American business development in the twenty-first century. If a district finds such a teacher, the whole program often rests perilously on the health or career goals of the teacher maintaining the program.

School districts that want to give young people experiences in a variety of languages at the elementary or middle school level may not be able to offer full-time assignments in any language. Getting competent language instructors, difficult enough when searching for a full-time employee, can become an impossible task when the assignments are less than full time. Also, districts that employ full-time language teachers can find themselves locked into offering traditional languages because they would not have any assignments for teachers of these languages if they tried to switch to Chinese, Japanese, Russian, or some other non-conventional language. They are reluctant to lay off conscientious staff who are long-term employees of the district.

Still another firm that has developed a niche market in public education is Sylvan Learning Systems. Though founded as a tutoring service the company established a contract educational service division in 1993 which, as of late 1995, operated on-site learning centers in twenty-three schools in five school districts including Baltimore; the District of Columbia; Dorchester and Talbot Counties in Maryland; and Pasadena, Texas. They recently acquired Remedial and Diagnostic Services Inc., a contract provider for parochial and private schools ("Private Firms," 1995).

Sylvan specializes in working with students who have been unsuccessful in school as well as those who need extra help to remain successful. They were natural allies for districts looking for help in working with students in Title I programs. The advantages of a private company in dealing with these special populations are no different from working with an elementary foreign language population. Rapid changes in the number of children to be served each year make it possible to expand and contract staff without the pain of layoffs of district staff, with all the tremors such a move induces throughout the whole teaching staff. Working with a firm that has a strong technology capacity and that has built a business in serving students who have special needs or problems in learning offers a higher probability of success than attempting the difficult task of identifying teachers who enjoy working with such students and the expensive task of keeping them trained and up-to-date with technology in serving such students. Also, there is the presence of clear accountability. If the company is unsuccessful in achieving defined goals, it can be terminated at the end of a contract.

There are many other companies emerging to service niche markets in the gigantic education industry. It is not the purpose of this book to summarize the services of all such companies. It should also be noted, however, that in addition to well-known companies and corporations expanding to service public education, there is a growing number of teachers who consider themselves "private practice" instructors. These are individuals who can contract directly with school districts, with companies serving education, or with parents to provide instructional services to students. In fact, in 1990 the American Association of Educators in Private Practice (AAEPP) was founded by a group of educators in Wisconsin to share ideas and support each other (Beales, 1995). Private practice teachers should not be thought of as professional rejects. They operate in this way for many reasons: family considerations (small children, the need to travel frequently with a spouse, etc.), the desire to be essentially free of bureaucratic supervisors, the desire to profit personally from creative teaching techniques, and the ability to control the content one teaches and/or the environment in which one is assigned to teach. Robin Gross, director of Maryland-based Science Encounters, a firm that focuses on hands-on science education for elementary age children and which now employs thirty part-time teachers, chose to become a private vendor of instructional services because "I didn't want to do yard duty. I didn't want to attend teacher conferences. I just wanted to teach science" (O'Leary and Beales, 1994, p. 40).

Employing a privately contracted teacher can also be an appropriate strategy for school districts with special needs. For example, there are retired science teachers or those who operate as private practitioners who have developed special curriculum modules that would ordinarily be beyond the capacity of regular elementary classroom teachers, who might not have sufficient expertise in science to design and teach a similar unit. The unit may require specialized equipment not available in the ordinary classroom. It might take too much time for the classroom teacher to design and set up the module. Of course, the advantages of curriculum enhancement of this kind are not limited to science. All kinds of curriculum enrichment are possible through contracted service; for example, specialized reading instruction, mathematics, and the fine and performing arts.

Many districts are probably already involved in contracting with one particular class of "private practice" professionals: coaches for athletic teams. As faculties have aged, many teachers having started their careers during the "baby boom" 1960s, it has become more and more difficult to find classroom teachers willing to work after school as coaches for low pay. This problem has been compounded by the rapid growth of athletic programs for females. Therefore, school districts have been contracting with individuals who work in the private sector or who are full-time homemakers to coach school teams or advise one or more co-curricular activities such as debate teams, yearbooks, and the like. Recognition of this phenomenon reduces the idea of contracting with a private entity to a more routine decision, one of degree rather than of kind.

COMPREHENSIVE EDUCATIONAL SERVICE CONTRACTING: THE EMO

The possibility of a full-fledged, privately sponsored challenge to public education disappeared, at least for a while, when Chris Whittle's telecommunications empire crashed into bankruptcy. The goal of Whittle's Edison Project to create a system of investor supported private schools that would compete with public schools was suddenly cut back sharply. In its redesigned form the Edison Project declares that its intention is to "form partnerships with schools in a variety of communities—small, urban, rural and suburban" but not to "manage all the schools in a community because we believe parents and staff should always have the freedom to choose from a variety of educational designs" (McGriff, 1995, p. 16). Given the abrupt turnaround in the company's focus, the public can decide whether the change is the result of a new vision or a set of interests being converted into principles. Nevertheless, the company is committed to contracting for the total instructional program of its client schools.

One of the largest of the firms focused on managing whole schools and school districts, sometimes called Education Management Organizations (EMOs), is also the longest established: Education Alternatives Inc. (EAI), based in Minneapolis, Minnesota. Created in 1986, EAI offers to provide not only educational services to schools or school districts but also, sometimes in partnership with KPMG Peat Marwick, Johnson Controls, National Bus Company and/or Computer Curriculum Corporation, it seeks to take over almost total operational responsibility for the school or district. This consortium asserts that, through efficiencies in management and building operations, the use of technology, and a custom designed curriculum, it can improve student achievement and also make a profit while operating with the same per pupil allotment as the district regularly receives. Though it operates no districts or schools as of this writing—its contracts with the Hartford, Connecticut School District and the Baltimore Public Schools were terminated because the districts refused to make payments EAI maintained were due to the firm—its financial assets, its partnerships with other private companies, and a new contract to operate up to 12 charter schools in Arizona suggest it is too soon to write its obituary.

There is no credible statistical evidence to support a claim that EAI was improving learning in the Baltimore, Maryland, public schools after several years of operation. (None of EAI's contracts ever lasted long enough to demonstrate substantial improvements in learning.) However, there was considerable subjective testimony that schools operated by EAI were cleaner, brighter, and technologically richer than they had been before the company came in.

It is both the honor and cross of this company to have entered into contracts in many urban environments, which present unique challenges to improving student learning. The company also endures the opposition of the resident labor union—usually the American Federation of Labor (AFL) affiliate in big cities—because, like most companies that enter an education environment, a first step by the vendor is to address the existing high cost of labor. In Baltimore, EAI eliminated the existing high-cost classroom aides, virtually all of whom were without a college degree, and replaced them with lower-cost interns who had degrees. All of these dismissed aides were members of the American Federation of Teachers (AFT) local unit. Chapter 7 will discuss in depth the issues related to the politics of privatization.

WHY AN EMO?

One of the most important questions that can be addressed by this publication is the motivation for school districts to look to Edison, EAI, or other companies to take over their education program, in whole or in part. It is relatively easy to understand why it makes sense for a school district to fill a niche with a teacher or citizen, who is a private contractor, or a company when such a solution is really the only one available or when the economic or educational advantages of taking such a step are obvious to almost everyone. But why would a school district reach out to a private company to perform the services for which staff have been fully trained to provide themselves? So far the answer has often been found in a desperation on the part of the district brought on by both fiscal and educational deficits.

In Washington, D. C., the district was millions of dollars in debt for operations during the 1995–1996 year alone. Superintendent Franklin L. Smith indicated that it "has half a billion dollars worth of deferred maintenance" (Schmidt, 1994, p. 28). In such dire financial conditions, finding dollars to make educational or facility improvements is almost impossible. So it is understandable that the district was willing to contract with a firm that had pledged to spend $850,000–1,000,000 on facility changes that would remain even if the contract were terminated. In Hartford students had the lowest scores of any district on state assessment tests. Here the initiative to bring in a private company came from board members who seemed to doubt that professional educators really had the expertise necessary to educate the students of the district. Like most urban school districts they also lacked sufficient funds to mount a major school improvement effort.

In Mt. Clemens, Michigan, one of the four sites in which the Edison Project was operating schools in 1995–1996, the school board president opined that "If public schools were a private business, they would be sued and out of business" (*Detroit News,* January 21, 1996). In Wilkinsburg, Pennsylvania, a suburb of Pittsburgh, only a third of the students score above the national median on standardized tests, though it has the highest tax rate in the county. After a review of five proposals to run Turner School, one of the district's elementary buildings, the board chose Alternative Public Schools of Nashville. This was the first school management contract for this company. For the same cost per child the company promised a longer school year, a longer school day, and teacher compensation linked to student performance.

Constructive Competition and Innovation

Is desperation the only justification for working with a private contractor for comprehensive instructional services? Probably not. Any organization tends to develop its own culture, a culture that more powerfully than a master contract or a school district policy book defines what behaviors are viewed as acceptable in the hearts and minds of employees. A culture inimical to innovation can stifle even the most energetic and innovative teacher or administrator. Even an organization that sees itself as open to change can hide a pathology not observable to those who go to work there every day. For example, districts that have great pride in their reputation for excellence and innovation can become hostile to any techniques and strategies that are not "home grown," especially if developed in a district they consider inferior to their own.

Employing a corporation to manage a school can foster innovation and provide a psychological challenge to even the best staff members to meet or exceed the results of the corporation. Even though the relationship between the Baltimore Public Schools and EAI was torn apart by disagreements over payment disputes, Walter Amprey, superintendent of the district, said he would enter into such a contract again, since he felt the presence of EAI fundamentally altered the culture of the district and sharpened the focus of teachers on student learning.

One school administrator described a desire on the part of his district to offer middle school students an opportunity to become exposed to instruction in the Japanese language. Berlitz Jr. was hired to teach the language. The teachers' union objected strenuously, insisting that a teacher or teachers should be hired by the district for this purpose, without any evidence that Japanese language teachers were available to the district. It was finally agreed that a district language teacher would be available in the class while the privately contracted teacher was working. The administrator indicated that, despite the initial uproar, the district language teachers eventually admitted that they had learned a lot by watching the techniques utilized by the Berlitz teacher. They soon began to use some of these techniques in their own instruction.

"OUTSOURCING" BY PRIVATE BUSINESSES

Examples and anecdotes described in this chapter have attempted to demonstrate that the real issue for schools in dealing with contracting with a private supplier is not a "public or private" decision but a "make or buy " choice. This has been a significant issue for private businesses for a long period of time, perhaps because they are always driven by the need to remain profitable if they are to stay in business. They would inevitably feel the need to respond quickly and creatively to a money losing food venture or a technologically weak data processing center.

Significant capital investment might not bring about proportionate productivity improvements that other, perhaps larger, firms were achieving through the purchase of hardware and software. Outsourcing, "the assignment of specific work to a third party for a specific length of time with an agreed upon price and service level" (Anderson, 1995), becomes a perfectly logical solution. Divesting the business of a money losing food service program or an inefficient data processing operation becomes not only good business but a necessary choice if a firm is to survive and compete.

As Ascher has noted,

> Contracting out in the public sector and outsourcing in the private sector are much like fraternal twins. . . . Both have resulted from changes in economic relationships and in the economy as a whole and both share similar motives: maximizing flexibility and responsiveness while minimizing cost. Far from a public or private issue, reliance on market solutions is a public and private development, and one which can only be evaluated against an economic—not a political—standard. (Kemp, 1991, p. 301)

The growing popularity of outsourcing some non-strategic functions in the private sector can be demonstrated by examining food service operations, one of the non-mission related functions school districts are considering for privatization.

The Marriott Corporation has summarized its estimate of the number of entities that are turning over food service functions to outside suppliers (Figure 3.1) (Beales and O'Leary, 1994):

Business	94%
Higher education	65%
Health care facilities	48%
School district	11% (est.)

In October, 1995 *Forbes* magazine published a 46-page special advertising supplement regarding outsourcing. They noted that: "No one in today's world believes that corporations should do everything themselves. . . (However) we live in an era of Total Quality and Total Customer satisfaction, and CEOs are loathe to rely on anyone else to perform any function in which less than acceptable quality could result. But in reality do they have a choice?" (Anderson, 1995, p. 4).

This is the same question that confronts public school officials. They may have evidence that a function or service currently delivered by government workers could be provided more cost efficiently by an

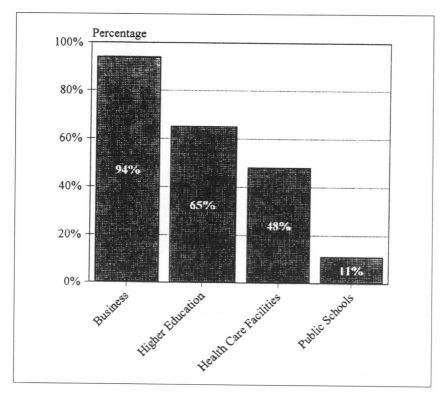

Figure 3.1. *The Marriott Corporation's Estimate of the Percent of Entities Privatizing Food Services.*

outside provider without a loss of quality. But they are not certain. If a private company turns over its food service operation to an outside provider and, despite its best efforts to define a standard of quality in the contract that the vendor must meet, the food proves unsatisfactory, officials have a temporary problem with employee morale until the problem is fixed or the contract is terminated. If a school board contracts its food service operation to a private company and the food is seen as unsatisfactory to students, the district can have a community uproar on its hands. And it will have gone through an often bruising struggle to terminate its employees to accomplish this embarrassing result.

SUMMARY

Contracting as a form of privatization has a long history in both the private and governmental sectors. As private businesses take more seriously the advice of management theorists that they should, as Peter Drucker has said, "know what business you are in," contracting has become increasingly popular in the private sector as companies strive to reduce costs and stay competitive in world markets. Government entities do not move into contracting out services quite so readily since terminating employees has significant community, labor relations, and political ramifications for local school districts. However, private sector involvement in delivering support services continues to grow, and in recent years companies have moved aggressively into the core function of public education—instruction.

The decision to employ a privately owned company to provide services in a school district should be made only after a careful consideration of the consequences of such a move to students, staff, and the community.

CHAPTER 4

Choosing a Make or Buy Solution

March 18, 1994

Mr. John T. Golle
Chairman and Chief Executive Office
Education Alternatives, Inc.
Minneapolis, MN 55431

Dear Mr. Golle:

We represent Taxpayers for Responsible Spending, a community group in the Pinckney School District. We have one mission: to get EAI out of Pinckney. We will fight you through any and every means possible. At last night's standing room only Board meeting over 400 community members stood against you. Not one stood for you. . . . This is only the beginning. . . . EAI cannot succeed in Pinckney without community support. . . . We vow that we will not stop fighting until you are gone.

(Excerpts from an actual letter.)

INTRODUCTION

A recent study of privatization conducted by the National School Boards Association (NSBA, 1995) found that 45% of the 354 responding school districts (Figure 4.1) looked to cost reduction as their main motivation to consider privatizing a service. This was twice the number of districts that expressed interest in contracting for management effi-

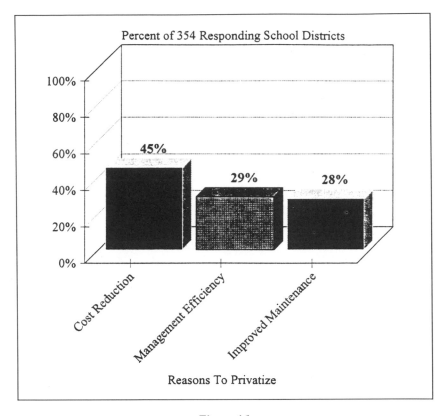

Figure 4.1.

ciency (29%) or improved maintenance of buildings (28%), the second and third ranked reasons to look to the private sector. Interestingly a survey by Touche Ross of every United States city with a population of more than 5,000 and every county with a population of more than 25,000, with a return rate of 19%, found that 74% of the officials expected privatization to achieve cost savings, a much larger percentage than school officials (Touche Ross, 1987).

While only one-third of the school district respondents to this study actually recorded a cost saving, Hilke's research (n.d.) concluded that "more than 100 studies over the course of the last 20 years have demonstrated privatization/competition cost savings" in non-school re-lated government services "from airport operation to weather forecast-ing" (p. 2). This somewhat disappointing statistic for schools may be largely attributable to the failure of districts to do a careful cost study before they became involved in a contract with a private vendor. The purpose of this chapter is to recommend some areas of district operations that should receive detailed analysis before deciding whether a contract with a private firm will be advantageous to the district.

FALSE OPTIONS

A school district concerned about its cost structure, the performance quality of district employees, or both, may jump to the conclusion that the only alternative is complete privatization of the program or service. This false assumption is naturally encouraged by the sales staff of private companies since it is their responsibility to sell jobs or at least position the company to make a bid or proposal on school district business. The district may find its assumption confirmed when bids to deliver the service are returned and the proposed fee is lower than the district's present costs. There are several logical fallacies that can entice a board into a bad decision.

The Quick Fix

The district may be misled by looking at the economics of privatization with only a short time frame, the period of the first contract. Once district employees have been sloughed off and a private company has come in, the vendor is better positioned to significantly increase fees for the next contract with the knowledge that the district will be reluctant to go back to providing a service that was recently privatized, since there are serious political ramifications in the community for such an action. Also, once a company has been established in the district for a few years, it has amortized many capital and other fixed costs. Thus the incumbent vendor is positioned to underbid other companies but still propose a significant increase in fees.

For example, a school district that is hurting financially may find it highly attractive to get out of the busing business, since it may find that its cost structure for labor may be high, and it can sell off its bus fleet to the vendor for a quick, one-time-only infusion of cash. Of course once the buses are gone, it is prohibitively expensive to replace this equipment should the contract prove unsuccessful. Now the only choice left to the district is to select from among several private vendors. The district may be trapped into a higher cost structure than it imagined when it signed the first contract. Therefore, one first false option is to view the possible advantages of privatization from a very narrow time frame.

The Either/Or Fallacy

Another false dichotomy that may present itself to the district is the notion that its only choice is to continue in the business of providing the service directly or get out of the business in favor of a private company. Neither choice may represent the best solution for the district's situation.

Ted Kolderie (1985) has noted that a decision to contract is not a simple one; it involves a large number of options. The contracting agency may do any of the following:

- contract for an indefinite period
- contract for a limited time with competition for renewal
- subdivide a task into subcontracts bid separately
- contract part of a function and maintain the other part "in-house"
- contract for personnel services only and maintain ownership of facilities and equipment
- contract for facilities and equipment and hire labor
- contract only for services that are highly specialized and used infrequently (e.g., legal and architectural services)
- operate mission specific services and contract for support services

Municipal governments, which have privatized services to a larger extent and probably for a longer period of time than schools, have often concluded that it is a bad idea to remove the municipality completely from a service. Therefore, some have divided up a jurisdiction into areas and obtained bids on the delivery of service in one or several of these areas. There are several advantages to this approach. First of all, the governmental entity doesn't get out of the business completely. It maintains a capacity to take back a privatized area on short notice. Second, it creates a real competitive environment for both the public employees and the private company. Each is under pressure to provide higher quality service for lower costs. If the private company is able to do a demonstrably better job, it can have the opportunity to have its territory expanded. If the public employees do a better job, they can drive out the private company. Normally the citizen is the winner, getting better service for less cost.

This is not really a new idea in schools either, just not a commonly implemented one. One of the authors worked in a large school district in New Jersey where about 60% of the busing services was provided by district employees. The other 40% of the district's bus transportation service was split among several small private companies. By improving its comparative position based on fees and performance, each of these entities was able to expand its share of the transportation pie. The Private Sector Task Force on Management and Productivity (1996) study of the Philadelphia School District's school support operations, completed at the request of Superintendent David Hornbeck, urged the district, which had an extremely high per pupil cost for transportation compared to other large city school districts, to "realign the relationship between contract and in-house operations to create a competitive environment for providing transportation; expand bus contract operations where it is cost effective" (p. T-6).

Another approach to avoiding an unnecessary either/or choice is to allow district employees to make a bid in competition with the private vendors. In *Reinventing Government,* Osborne and Gaebler (1992) recount a number of anecdotes about municipal fire departments and sanitation staff winning all or part of a bid requested by a municipality. In addition to keeping their jobs, these former municipal employees now had the chance to profit by their labor and their ideas. In one situation employees got to keep 10% of the savings generated by any of their ideas (p. 77). In 1989 the ARA Corporation suggested to the Phoenix, Arizona, school district that they could reduce the district's costs for cafeteria services and requested a four-year contract to prove their argument. District cafeteria staff suggested that the company be given a one-year contract in two high schools as a pilot to compare ARA's performance with the in-house program, which would continue to operate in two other high schools. After one year the in-district program had higher profits and fewer complaints about food, and the board decided to terminate the agreement with the private contractor. The district had achieved its goal of assuring the best quality for the money paid without running the risk of both community turmoil and an expensive mistake (National Education Association, 1995a).

The Surplus Staff Syndrome

A careful scrutiny of personnel issues can unmask significant residual costs that might burden the district after a contract is signed with a vendor. Whether a district engages the Edison Project, which will work only with the support of the teachers and their union, or Alternative Public Schools, a Nashville based company which insists on the right to replace teachers in any school it operates, there will be spin-off effects on teacher staffing for the district. When Alternative Public Schools rejects some teachers in a school for which it is responsible or when teachers previously assigned to a school now associating with the Edison Project decide not to stay there, a district can end up with more teachers than it needs. Such extra staff can seriously distort the economics of a contract with a private company. In Wilkinsburg, the district has been ordered by the court to reinstate with back pay teachers laid off as a result of the Alternative Public Schools demand.

Student Momentum Gain

Another area that requires some scrutiny is the past performance of students who might be attending a school proposed to be taken over by a private company. Private companies sometimes base their sales argument on a promise to improve learning and attendance in the schools for which they are responsible. A school with a significant number of students who are below average on various standardized measures of achievement may well be already in an improving mode. The district ought to look at achievement data on a longitudinal basis. The district could end up paying a company for achievement that would have occurred anyway since the present staff had positioned the school toward continuous improvement.

ALTERNATIVES TO PRIVATIZATION

School board members are, by definition, policymakers whose prime responsibility is to focus on strategic issues that contribute to student success. They are elected to assure that services are provided efficiently and competently. They need not insist that the district own and operate the means to produce all services. Money strapped school districts cannot afford to overlook any methods that might help to deliver more results for the money spent.

However, experience shows that all the alternatives, including *internal solutions*, must be examined before awarding a contract to a private vendor. Failure to consider all internal alternatives will expose board members to valid criticism. Conversely, board members who are viewed as carefully considering all the options will likely have the support of the general public as they go about the task of trying to focus scarce dollars on instructional improvement.

Conducting an analysis of the strengths, weaknesses, opportunities, and threats (SWOT Analysis) presented by the option of privatizing will provide the district with the knowledge necessary for good decision making. Figure 4.2 demonstrates an analysis of the possibility of hiring a private company to provide school transportation services.

Even a cursory examination of this analysis suggests that a quick move to contracting transportation services could involve serious long-term dangers to the district. Some of the options listed below might well improve the cost effectiveness and cost efficiency of the service as currently provided by district staff and not require some of the risks described in the SWOT assessment.

Consultation

No one staff member ever has all the necessary knowledge to carry out job responsibilities at the maximum level of efficiency and effective-

---

Strengths of the Proposal

1. The company has a long history of successfully providing school transportation services including a five year history in a neighboring district.
2. The district may be able to reduce transportation costs 15%, well beyond the policy threshold that board policy requires before privatization will be considered.

Weaknesses of the Proposal

The company does not wish to bid on transportation for co-curricular activities.

Opportunities

Contracting out transportation enables the district to achieve a cash infusion of $45,000 through the sale of some of the district's buses to the company.

Threats

The district could be vulnerable after the initial contract expires if service has not been satisfactory because there would be insufficient funds to purchase another fleet of buses, and there do not appear to be other private companies that would bid on the contract.

Figure 4.2. Hypothetical SWOT Analysis.

ness. One approach to drawing on the knowledge base of others is to hire a private firm to come to the district, analyze operations, and make recommendations to improve effectiveness and reduce costs. In large metropolitan areas such companies may be readily available and, though not inexpensive, may return their fees in one year of improved operations. They may even be willing to make their fees a percentage of savings achieved as a result of their recommendations. As noted above, the Philadelphia School District was able to get the help of the private sector in analyzing the cost efficiency and effectiveness of its school support operations (transportation, facilities, human resources, food service, and management information systems) without cost by appealing to the sense of civic responsibility of its corporate citizens.

Almost everywhere it is not uncommon for "job alike" school groups to meet monthly, quarterly, or semi-annually to share ideas and participate in training. An invitation to one or more colleagues from other districts to visit and examine operations can produce positive results for no costs or minimal expenditures for mileage and meals.

Budget Targeting

Once a delivery system has been running for a period of time workers become comfortable with it and usually feel that they are performing successfully. Thus they are reluctant to change procedures. One method of forcing change within the system is to set financial targets for the delivery of a service and work with employees to discover ways to meet those targets. For example, if a contract with a private transportation company is likely to reduce operating costs by 15%, staff can be asked for suggestions that will achieve economies of that magnitude within the district's operations and/or to define different service levels that might bring a saving equal or close to the desired target figure. Budget targeting is a variation of the technique of allowing local employees to bid against private vendors to deliver the service.

Collaborative Efforts

When geography permits, collaboration with other districts, other governmental bodies, and non-profit agencies can enable partners to share staff and facilities and thereby reduce costs. There are several approaches to establishing collaborations:

- joining with another school district to share facilities or staff; for example, one district agreeing to service buses from other districts at its repair facilities for a fee
- joining with another governmental entity to provide a service (One of the authors worked in a school district that provided mainframe computer services through a facility jointly paid for by the school district and the township.)
- creating a joint powers authority to provide a service to all participant districts with one district serving as fiscal agent and employer of record
- calling on the regional education service agency, if one exists, to provide a service on behalf of districts willing to co-fund the effort
- working with one or more non-profit agencies to provide a service all need, for example, food service, snow removal, grounds maintenance, and the like

Collaborative arrangements among educational institutions provide the advantage that current employees are able to continue on the rolls of one of the school districts, thereby maintaining their government retirement privileges and the same level of salary and fringe benefits. Because per capita employee costs may not change in any of these arrangements, the primary savings from these options comes from reductions in the size of the work force. Though the savings may not be as great as can be achieved through privatization, these cost saving efforts are likely to be much less politically volatile within the community than the complete sloughing off of district employees, many of whom undoubtedly live in the district and who can marshal a vigorous public objection to contracting with a private vendor. That is the pragmatic justification for maintaining a public solution. There may be a principled justification as well; that is, that no one class of employees ought to bear the burden of the district's financial problems.

POOR COST ANALYSIS

School districts sometimes err by too quickly jumping to the conclusion that privatization is the appropriate solution to their cost or quality problems. It is, however, much more likely that districts will conclude that privatization is *not* a solution for them because of failure to capture the real costs of operating a service themselves. Savas (1987, p. 259) has suggested that the cost of in-house delivery of a service is frequently underestimated by as much as 30%. Robert O'Neill, a principal in the Sacramento, California, office of KPMG Peat Marwick and author of the California study, *Handbook for Identifying and Analyzing Pupil Transportation Costs and Contracting from Pupil Transportation Services,* notes that districts can easily underestimate the cost of their transportation program by 25% (Finkel, 1991).

A 1987 study (Mercer/Slavin) of the contracting practices of 120 cities, counties, and special district governments found that 50% of the respondents reported having no formal methodology for conducting cost comparisons. It is not likely that the situation is much improved today. There is also no reason to believe that school districts are any more effective at authentic cost analysis than their local government colleagues.

Cost analysis is a very complicated issue that cannot easily be summarized so as to apply to a variety of functions and services. A contributing cause of this difficulty is the differing accounting methods used to track costs and expenditures applicable to the public and private sector. Private businesses use accrual accounting while public entities use modified accrual accounting as the norm. This difference becomes especially important when attempting to make comparisons of capital assets and acquisitions.

Invariably, private companies will depreciate an asset on the books over its normal period of use. As an example, if the bus has a normal useful life of ten years, the value of the bus will be carried on the books for a decade, at a 10% lower rate each year. School districts, on the other hand, will expense the full cost of a school bus in the year it is purchased. Without carrying that depreciating asset on the books, it appears that the district has no cost for the bus in any year but the year it is purchased. When the bus has to be replaced, the total cost of the bus will hit the books in the year of purchase. Therefore, comparing capital costs of public and private entities can lead to distorted conclusions.

Since both California and New York State, as well as the National School Boards Association (Taggart, 1990), have published studies of transportation costs, the example of cost analysis demonstrated here will be drawn from the school busing function. Conclusions in that area can suggest the broad range of issues that need to be addressed when attempting to determine actual local costs of other services such as food service programs, buildings and grounds operations, and so forth.

Calculating Direct Costs

Martin (undated) and others have noted that the full costs of a service can only be calculated by adding up *all* direct and indirect costs. Edney and O'Neill (1990) have suggested that the costs of operating a fifty school bus transportation system can be underestimated by as much as $600,000 if all direct and indirect costs are not included in the district's calculation.

The direct costs that are easiest to capture are those that can be fully attributed to a function. They would include the items listed in Figure 4.3.

Salaries paid to bus drivers are obviously direct costs, since it is easy to attribute bus driver salaries to the school transportation function. If some bus drivers are also employed by the district in some other capacity—custodian, lunch room aide, classroom paraprofessional—when not driving a school bus, then the calculation becomes more complicated, especially if workers are salaried rather than hourly employees. But the calculation is not difficult. If the individual spends three of eight working hours driving a bus, then 37.5% of the total salary is attributable to the cost of running the transportation function. Obviously the calculation is even easier if bus drivers are paid an hourly rate. If all transportation costs are lumped together, but the district is trying to determine actual transportation costs for general education, athletics and co-curricular activities, handicapped students, and other discrete areas, an allocation factor can be applied to direct costs based, for example, on miles traveled for each function. "If general education transportation accounts for 92% of all mileage, that percentage would be applied to driver wages" (Finkel, 1991). Separating costs this way permits bid specifications that call for separate bid prices for each of these functions. Such an analysis might reveal that transportation of general education students is best provided by the district but the less frequent types of transportation are better handled by a contractor.

There are other direct costs that are not always included in the cost calculation, an omission that can seriously distort the district's real costs. All of the fringe benefit and retirement expenses should be allocated to the transportation function. Interest on bonds and loans floated to support

Readily Perceived Costs

Wages of drivers, managers, substitutes, repair staff
Fringe benefit costs
Fuel purchase costs
Consumables (tires, oil, filters, hoses, antifreeze, etc.)
Equipment purchases
Lease/rental costs for facility/equipment

Often Overlooked Costs

Insurance
   liability
   property and casualty
   workers compensation
Utilities
   water
   electric
   telephone
   natural gas
Inventory
   fuel
   supplies
   parts
Office supplies and furnishings
Maintenance of facility and equipment
Cost of capital
   bus depreciation
   interest costs on building vehicles and facilities
   facility maintenance, repair, and replacement

Figure 4.3. Direct Costs.

a function fully must also be included as a direct cost. Examples of such costs might include the charge to a bond issue of the cost of building a bus garage/repair facility or acquiring new buses. If the district is using a full accrual accounting system, it could depreciate the value of capital assets like buildings and buses just as a private company would. Substitute and standby drivers, leasing costs, furniture, office supplies, radios, and other operating expenses directly related to transportation must also be included.

Utility and Inventory Costs

Utility costs of buildings assigned a singular function may also be hard to capture at first since they may be aggregated into a district account for utilities. Obviously the bus garage and repair facility use a certain amount of heat, light, water, and telephone service. Yet it may take a little work to derive some numbers for these costs. Here again costs might be estimated by allocation. For example, if the district's transportation facilities constitute 10% of the total district floor space, then a 10% allocation of costs of each of the utilities may be a reasonable way to approximate these costs.

Still another expense, "almost always unaccounted for, is the cost of holding an inventory of parts and fuel . . . another example of opportunity costs" (Taggart, 1990) that should be included in the cost analysis when determining district costs to provide transportation service.

Opportunity Costs

Even if the district does not depreciate an asset over time, it should consider the "opportunity costs" of a capital asset; that is, the value of property if it were not needed for its current use. For example, if the district has ten school buses that will not be sold to a contracting company, the buses still have value in that they might be sold or leased to the municipal recreation department, a senior citizens apartment building, or some other entity that might be able to make use of a school bus. If each bus could be sold for $5,000, the district forfeits $50,000 in lost opportunity costs by keeping the buses operating for school services.

Non-Salary Personnel Cost

In order not to exaggerate district costs it is important to review budgeted positions to be sure that no vacancies are being carried on the books that have not been filled for a while or that the district would have no intention of filling in the foreseeable future if it were to continue to provide the service itself (National Education Association, 1995a).

Overtime costs can be another critical issue. It is important to adopt a method that regularizes overtime costs to avoid distortions for anomalous events; for example, a winter that has had an excessive amount of snow. Local costs for maintenance and operations costs could be misrepresented by a one-year view of this account. It would be wise, perhaps, to compute an average of several years when determining the district's ordinary overtime costs. It would also be important to ascertain how a prospective private vendor might be planning to treat overtime costs. Are they included in the base bid, no matter how high they may go in a given year? Is the district going to be billed for overtime costs that exceed the overtime costs included in the bid amount?

Indirect Costs

Indirect costs are a far more complex issue, and two quite separate views are possible about the attribution of these costs.

Indirect costs are those that are attributable to more than one function or service. They are not directly attributable to one particular activity—in this illustration, bus transportation. For example, the payroll department may have the responsibility for calculating and printing the payroll checks of school transportation personnel, but there is no line item in the budget of the payroll clerk specifically attributable to its service to the transportation department. The accounts payable clerk is responsible for cutting checks to cover purchases made by the transportation department for gasoline, bus tires, engine parts, and so forth. It costs money to carry out these services and therefore a precise accounting system would allocate a proportionate share of the costs of these support services to the transportation function. Other costs attributable to the transportation function include printing, delivery services, building maintenance, office supplies, postage, and utilities.

Some districts, when doing cost comparisons, recognize the logic of attributing indirect costs to the function under study and make a comprehensive calculation when attempting to determine the total costs to the district of providing a particular service. That is, they attempt to prorate many of the same costs listed under direct costs—salaries, benefits, pensions, etc.—that are attributable to the support services that assist transportation and other functions. Thus, some portion of the fringe benefit, retirement, and other costs of the central office payroll clerk will be charged to the transportation service.

Others argue that this is an artificial statistic, one which will inflate the size of the district's cost figure and misrepresent the true financial picture of the district. They argue that in private business, especially big business, it may be possible to reduce the size of a department when one of these functions is removed or to transfer some people to other departments and thereby achieve actual reduced cost reductions when contracting out a service. Therefore, real savings in indirect costs are achieved. However, they insist that most public school districts are too small to achieve real cost savings when a function is removed. The district will still need a payroll clerk and an accounts payable clerk. It will be unrealistic to consider reducing the assignment of a dedicated worker from full- to part-time. Intradistrict transfers are impractical and politically unpopular.

Each district will have to decide this issue for itself. However, it must be recognized that an unwillingness to make changes in staffing when one or more functions is removed is to forego another "opportunity" and therefore the district does incur a cost, whether it wishes to count it or not.

Transitional Costs

Experienced school administrators and board members recognize that only in Wonderland would it be possible for a district to drop a service one day and have it picked up by a private contractor the next without any additional costs of achieving this transition. Careful planning and "worst case" scenario writing may be the wisest approach to estimating these costs. Two related items are particularly relevant to a cost analysis: legal fees and one-time-only labor costs that may derive from collective bargaining.

It is pointed out elsewhere in this book that there are several primary legal issues which must be carefully explored. Of course the first question to be researched is the legal authority of the board of education to contract for one or another services. A mistake here could be an expensive calamity for the district.

Other, equally important, questions to be considered relate to labor issues that can have a high price tag, either because failure to do appropriate background work can end up in expensive litigation or because there are some special costs that can easily be overlooked in a transition situation (Marcel, 1994):

- Is the district prohibited from contracting during the term of its current labor agreement; that is, must it wait until the current contract expires to begin the contracting negotiation?
- Does state law require that a switch to contracting be a subject of bargaining, whether a contract is in force or not?
- What is the value of accumulated vested benefits of the employees?

- Are there any likely claims for unemployment insurance by employees not hired by the contracting company?
- Do employees who are hired by the company have any claims to unemployment benefits during the summer of the first year of transition?

Though these transition costs are likely to be one-time-only expenses, they can be proportionately very high if the contract is likely to be a short one, and there is no clear conviction that the relationship with a private partner can be counted on to last a long time.

Rehabilitation Costs

There are some costs that do not directly affect the cost comparison of providing a service directly or contracting for its provision. Nevertheless, these costs ought to be estimated and kept on the table as cost comparison is taking place. The most significant of these would be the costs resulting from termination of a contract with an unsatisfactory vendor and the obligation to return to providing the service with district employees, probably because there are no viable alternate service providers. This is not a serious worry for cafeteria services (the kitchens will still be there) or with maintenance and operations services because a major capital investment would not be necessary to return to cleaning buildings and caring for grounds. But, as already noted, once buses are sold, the district faces an enormous expense if it is necessary to go back into the busing business. The Pinckney School District faced this problem when the company with which it was contracting for transportation services, National Bus, was the target of purchase by Laidlaw. "It's very much of a bummer because there's no competition left," moaned the business manager (*Livingston County Press,* May 1, 1996).

Other Costs

The nature of many school support services makes them difficult to supervise closely. Bus drivers are on the road for most of their shift. Many custodians and maintenance workers are on duty during an afternoon shift when the principal is no longer on site. At best such workers operate under the direction of a "straw boss." It is not always easy to determine exactly the full range of activities carried out by each worker simply by looking at job descriptions. Thus, it is important that the district have a detailed listing of all of the tasks carried out by each employee so that these duties can be included in the expectations of a private contractor. Discovery of a large number of these undocumented tasks after a contract is bid can lead to more billings to the district by the vendor and seriously distort the cost comparison that justified the decision to contract.

Contracts with vendors are not self-policing. There are costs of assuring quality of work performance and contract compliance, including verifying the bills submitted by the vendor, dealing with dissatisfied citizens, etc. These costs are not always easy to quantify at the start of a relationship with a vendor, but the cost of staff time to deal with these issues must be allocated within the cost comparison.

Issues related to the cost of materials and supplies also need to be clarified. For example, if a company is going to take over the food service program, which party will have the financial obligation to supply and, perhaps more importantly, repair or replace kitchen equipment and service ware such as glasses, dishes, utensils, cash registers, etc?

Costs that might be related to interruptions of service, whether acts of God or not, need to be clarified. For example, the *New York Times* (February 9, 1996) reported that employees of a private company, contracted to provide custodial and maintenance services to eight schools in Brooklyn, walked off the job "leaving 10,000 students and their teachers without heat for several hours." Certainly a job action can occur when a service is under the direction of the school district, but a government operator has more flexibility in dealing with a problem in a service under its own control, including whatever additional costs might be incurred in dealing with the service interruption. Will a private company be willing to bear the costs of dealing with a job action? What guarantees are in the contract that it will respond promptly to maintain uninterrupted service to students?

Costing Methodology

Knowing all costs of a service does not guarantee a correct decision. The way the data is analyzed will affect the conclusions that are reached. Deficiencies in costing methodology can result from poor analysis techniques or from deliberate distortion by those doing the study. For example, when the Private Sector Task Force on Management and Productivity (1996) was examining the Philadelphia Public Schools' transportation system, district transportation officials maintained that they did not contract out more bus service because delivering it in-house was cheaper. However, after digging into the data presented by these administrators, Task Force members discovered that the district had "policies favoring in-house operations over private contractor options and assigning less efficient routes to contractors." Therefore, "the school district routes carry more students and involve shorter distances than contractor routes" (p. T-12).

A policy board and chief executive might deal with weaknesses in financial analysis, whether due to inadequate skill level or bias, by asking that the accounting firm responsible for the district's audit do the cost analysis of public versus private solutions or have the firm verify the work of school officials.

MAKING A DECISION

Good decisions about contracting are best made when the employer is clear about the goals to be achieved through privatization. At least publicly, most government officials declare that their interest in moving to contracting is driven by the need or desire to reduce costs. They are reluctant to openly declare another motive, such as a desire to get rid of current employees because of dissatisfaction with the job they are doing. A mutually bruising public conflict is likely to follow such accusations. However, other, more positive motives for privatizing have been suggested earlier:

- the need to acquire expertise that may not be needed full time (the common reason for retaining a law firm rather than hiring an attorney as a district employee)
- the need for special services not generally available (for example, obtaining a teacher of Chinese)
- the need to make significant capital investment to maintain a service in-house when such funds are not available (for example, the need to upgrade a data processing center)

Assuming, therefore, that cost savings are going to be the expressed motivation of a privatization initiative, a government body will want to define all the cost saving options open to it described earlier in this chapter before making a decision to privatize a service.

If none of these options proves attractive, feasible, or sufficient, the district can consider privatizing part, but not all, of the service if that is a realistic alternative. An example has already been given of a school district that contracted out bus transportation in several regions of the district to private companies. It might also be feasible to bid out food service or building and maintenance operations at elementary schools but not at the high school, and so forth. A variation on this "broken front" approach is to segregate the bid pieces so that at least two companies will receive part of the district's business. Obviously this increases the competition necessary to keep costs low and quality high (National School Boards Association, 1995).

The governing body also needs to decide in advance the size of cost reductions that will justify the difficulties of privatizing. For example, "the federal government, the state of Texas, and the city of Cincinnati, Ohio have all established a threshold level of 10% when considering a change from in-house to contract service delivery" (Martin, n.d., p. 12). Even short-term savings of a defined amount need to be weighed against the possible risks of entering into a contract that proves unsatisfactory when there are no alternate suppliers waiting to step forward or there is uncertainty whether other bidders would be quite as motivated to keep prices at the level of the original bidder.

There may also be some other factors that should be included in the decision-making process that have economic value but may not be subject to straightforward economic analysis. For example, in addition to whatever clear economic advantages may be involved in the bid of a school transportation vendor, the district may want to consider that it now may also have access to newer buses, a better trained repair staff, more sophisticated routing systems, and other features that have economic consequences but which may not appear on the balance sheet. Of course they could be included in a cost analysis if the district would consider these features necessary and would budget to acquire them if a contracted solution is not sought.

SUMMARY

Though the privatization movement seems driven by a need on the part of government agencies to save money, it is not the only option to reduce costs. A variety of intergovernmental and interagency options are also available.

However, a school district wanting to consider the option of privatizing will need specific, reliable data about the district's direct and indirect cost structure. This accounting for costs must also include "opportunity costs," the inability to use for educational purposes dollars that are tied up in inventory of some kind.

The examples in this chapter have been drawn largely from the field of school transportation because it is one of the most widely contracted functions—over 30% of all school transportation in the country (National School Boards Association, 1995) and over 40% in California (Edney & O'Neill, 1990). Because contracting is so large a piece of this important school service, and because school transportation vendors seem to have been more aggressive than their counterparts in other fields in promoting and publicizing the cost efficiencies of their services, the cost structure of transportation has been more widely studied in the educational literature and therefore examples from this literature have been discussed here.

However, all of the general concepts discussed for transportation apply, to a greater or lesser extent, to the other support services that might be privatized. For example, when analyzing the cost structure of the district's food service program, it is necessary to define and allocate such direct costs as utility bills and inventory. Indirect costs for services such as payroll processing, accounts payable, in-district transportation (especially if there are one or more central kitchens serving satellite schools), printing, and other necessary support structure must be captured.

CHAPTER 5

Moving toward Privatization: Roles and Responsibilities

Once the district dropped the privatizing bombshell, board meetings became spectacles. Over 400 school district residents and employees packed the high school cafeteria at the biweekly regularly scheduled meetings. These large, sometimes unruly, meetings became usual fare during the months of debate about privatizing. Tape recorders relentlessly whirred and TV cameras focused in and out on the participants.

The usually quiet board of education business meetings, which drew ten to fifteen observers, were only a memory. Although the number of tables made available to the press was expanded fourfold, they remained crammed with regional and national media reporters scribbling notes meeting after meeting. During recesses they buttonholed board members and the superintendent for comments that would hopefully be controversial or at least unique enough to be used as a mini scoop. At the same time, parents whose vested interest was the quality of their child's education and employees who believed that their jobs were on the line vied for community and media attention.

The public comment segment took a larger portion of each subsequent board meeting. The board's discussion of its official business consistently was denied the discussion time and breadth these action items needed. Meetings grew in length with important policy issues being decided by a mentally tired and physically exhausted board at one and two o'clock in the morning. Despite all the time invested, few new insights were gained from the repetitious harangues against privatizing, the company offering a contract, and board members interested in exploring the advantages of privatizing.

The veiled physical threats against the board required local and regional law enforcement to be visible in the parking lots. Undercover officers were assigned to monitor the meetings. In the local police chief's words, "It's better that we have 50 false alarms than miss the one time that our presence is needed."

This book is intended to assist all involved in a privatization debate to avoid the trauma that was associated with the real-world scenario described above. A similar drama does not inevitably have to be replayed in all school districts that investigate the potential benefits of private sector contracting.

WHY PRIVATIZE?

As reported earlier, the momentum for examining contracting with private companies is growing at an almost exponential rate in education. Concluding from over 300 school district responses to its research, the National School Boards Association (1995b) asserted, "School board members across the country are deliberating the benefits and drawbacks of contracts with private companies, and becoming informed purchasers of educational services in the marketplace. For many school boards, contracting with private companies expands the options they have in exercising leadership to best serve the students of their districts" (p. 1).

The current energy expended by other branches of government and private sector companies to "reengineer" their operations has increased the pressure on school boards to rethink and revise their view of learning and the learning environment. This corporate reengineering is mirrored in school districts as a self-renewing process forcing districts to engage in a review of what, how, and when learning occurs, and by whom and at what cost support for the learning environment is provided. It is the school board that is the responsible agent for articulating the policy that drives systemic reform and continuous improvement with the twin goals of efficiency and quality.

Fiscal austerity is pressuring districts to address the root causes of their systems' organizational inefficiencies. This growing demand to maximize the impact of each available dollar on student learning is fueling the pressure on school districts to use the private sector to provide both support services and instructional services. More and more boards are trying to identify which organizational structures and processes are most likely to yield success for all students. As they promise their constituents that dollars for education will be spent wisely, they are compelled to turn rhetoric into reality. This obligation, in turn, results in a willingness to consider which services can effectively be contracted to others. Unfortunately, the process used by some boards to examine action before planning and strategies before policy usually results in what should have been avoidable community turmoil described at the beginning of this chapter.

Although the most often cited benefit of privatizing services is the reduction of costs, other benefits of outsourcing service delivery are cited by districts (National School Boards Association, 1995b, p. 6):

- improved learning
- increased efficiency
- reduction of response time
- cost avoidance
- enhanced teacher/learning environment
- reduced employee absenteeism
- increased community involvement

Robert Roy, who became Pinckney superintendent as the privatization debate continued into a second school year, acknowledges that the district's money saving contract with a busing company has freed educators to focus on the district's primary mission—education. In public presentations he has noted (Roy, 1995) that

The district saves time because it no longer:
- negotiates union contracts
- handles Workers' Compensation claims
- calculates bus routes or handles the majority of complaints
- deals with alternate fuels, ADA requirements, environmental regulations, etc.
- sets bus specifications and bids fleet additions
- is held responsible for bus driver negligence
- maintains and improves the bus facility
- provides extensive bus driver training

Dr. Roy (1995) identifies additional benefits of contracting out the school transportation service:

- The company has become a district tax payer.
- State inspected fleet ratings have improved from "good" to "excellent."
- The safety accountability program now has continuous monitoring.
- The district's single limit body injury/property damage coverage has been increased from $5 million to $21 million per accident.

The need to at least consider privatization of district services appears clear. However, success in this endeavor seems directly related to careful planning about how to manage such a study. Stakeholders must have a clear idea about their roles in contributing to a well thought-out decision.

THE PRIVATIZATION STUDY: ROLES AND RESPONSIBILITIES

The School Board

Developing Policy

Policy development is the antecedent to a well-managed administrative process. As the venerable and often-quoted philosopher Yogi Berra is alleged to have said, "If you don't know where you are going, you may not get there." The school district's compass for action is the board's translation of their constituents' values into policy. The emotional stress that often accompanies a privatizing initiative will be minimized in those districts that clearly articulate these values and anchor in policy any decision to privatize.

School boards must ordinarily deliberate in the open, within the tangled context of complicated, frequently contradictory, federal and state policies. (The legal issues that impact the board's development of policy are discussed in later chapters.) As the board holds the public discussions that precede the coming to policy agreement, they engage in a reality test of their vision. Public discussions of vision and policy contribute to fostering an environment of trust. Mutual confidence, in turn, results in maintaining the social health of the district and, as a concomitant benefit, the political viability of board members.

There is little controversy about the primacy of the board's responsibility to develop policy and thereby set the plan of action for the district's operations. It is important for the board to focus on this essential role well before engaging in the debate about privatizing a particular function or the specifics of a company's contract offer. One of the more significant benefits of these publicly held policy discussions is that they usually provide a sufficient level of abstraction to permit the best chance for rational dialogue. Discussions about policy center on the need to provide for the greater good and usually avoid the specifics; i.e., the service that should be privatized, the cost of any particular contract, or other topics that ignite the fervor of special interests. Yet these policy statements must be specific enough to authorize a change in the conventional methods of providing programs and services. Once the policy has set the parameters permitting, or even fostering, alternatives that are inclusive of a privatizing activity, the inevitable question asked of the board—"Why are you privatizing this function?"—will have an answer.

As the board considers policy language, it should determine the specific reasons for privatizing the delivery of public service.

(1) *Improved Accountability:* The fundamental policy, as opposed to financial, argument in support of privatization will be, as it is now, the issue of accountability. Writer after writer has argued that public services are without accountability for several reasons: the lack of standards, the lack of a basis of comparison, and the lack of will or legal flexibility on the part of public boards to remedy poor work and terminate workers found unsatisfactory. When a service is privatized the board will, or at least should, establish performance standards for the contracting company. The very process of establishing standards will give districts an opportunity to reinvent their own desired standards of service.

Further, when a well-designed contract stipulates results that are tied to the level of remuneration and longevity of the contractual relationship, company employees become linked to the success or failure of the company. When a company fails to meet the requirements of the contract and the expectations of the board and its constituents, the company's existence is put at risk. This relationship challenges the company to work hard to achieve success by fulfilling the board's expectations.

(2) *Enhanced Cost Efficiency:* It is well recognized that large producers of goods and services have significant advantages over smaller producers. They can buy materials more cheaply because they buy in larger volume. They can sell their products or services at lower cost because they can make larger profits through increased volume. They can afford higher technology equipment, which increases their ability to produce higher quality at lower cost. They can afford to hire the most knowledgeable managers because their financial circumstances permit higher investment at the front end to get lower costs at the production/service end. They can afford the highest levels of training for their workers because fewer better trained workers can produce more than more less skilled workers.

Competition can also work to provide school districts with the most cost efficient service at the highest quality. When employees or companies provide services for which others may compete, a sense of job entitlement disappears. The company and its employees know that the board can turn to the competition for a better price or an improved quality of service.

(3) *Sharper Mission Focus:* Earlier reference was made to the comments of Paul Houston, executive director of the American Association of School Administrators (AASA), regarding the lack of special expertise of educators to provide support services (Houston, 1994, p. 133). If superintendents and their immediate assistants increasingly disengage from operating support services, they can increase their opportunity to focus on the main mission of the school district, student learning, and work to improve the delivery systems that will maximize student achievement. They are freed of the planning, logistical, labor relations, and daily problem solving issues involved in operating support services directly.

(4) *Innovative Thinking:* David Bennett, once EAI's president, believes that "Our current system is more likely to punish innovators and reward resisters. We need to reverse this tendency for the sake of our children" (Bennett, 1991, p. 37). Innovating simply to bring about new ways of doing things cannot be viewed as the ultimate goal of good management. But since the issuance of *A Nation at Risk,* school leaders have been searching for ways to achieve better academic performance and more economically delivered services. Innovation is enhanced when companies can survive only when they provide better quality and efficiency than their competition. As Tom Peters (1995) puts it, "The only sustainable competitive advantage comes from out-innovating the competition" (p. 130). Further, private companies can avoid the restraints of ideology, politics, and populism when making decisions about what works best within the available resources. Borden and Rauchut (1996) reaffirm this view: "Private markets open the door to change, innovation, redesign, imagination, and experimentation. Competition takes us into the future with a myriad of alternative answers to questions we haven't even asked yet, while central planning designs solutions to yesterday's problems" (p. 20).

With all these assumed advantages of privatization in mind the board can then begin to define a policy statement that interprets the community's values in regard to these issues. Listed below are the basic components of possible district policy statements related to privatizing:

- In order to maximize increasingly scarce resources the school district will continuously evaluate the cost effectiveness of all district support services and investigate options that might be available in the private sector to provide necessary services at a lower cost. A possible cost saving of ten percent or more will be the threshold for such an investigation.
- The district endeavors to provide as rich a curriculum as possible. When the existing teaching staff is unable to provide a board approved instructional program, the school district may hire private companies and/or teachers to offer less than full-time instruction in specialized subjects. Such instruction shall be evaluated annually. Contracts will be renewed yearly after all appropriately certified permanent staff have been offered the opportunity to teach the specialized class.
- In order to foster and maintain an instructional program of the highest quality the school district may hire a private sector company to manage one or more of the district's schools. The selected company must manage the school and its instructional program with the same or fewer dollars per pupil that are provided for the remainder of the district's students at the same level. The initial contract with such a private sector education management organization will be limited to three (3) years, thereafter renewable for four year terms.

Preparing the Staff and the Community

School boards must retain their role as the voice of the public regardless of the positions of their individual members on privatizing. When the board initiates change, especially when privatizing, members have the important responsibility to convince the staff and community that they will keep a careful eye on the innovation and that they will work to make it successful regardless of any member's belief.

Education is a labor intensive industry. Saving money in educational activities usually translates into reducing wages and benefits. Boards must evaluate whether a private company's change from district employee wages to competitive labor market standards (e.g., what a food server might earn in the private sector) is compatible with their community's ethos and the legal and regulatory environment in which the district operates. It is easy for boards to be accused of using private companies to undo overly generous contracts with employees as the primary motivation for outsourcing district services. Such a board motivation will not be constructive to achieving the district's mission. Few, if any, boards want to be viewed as fostering low wage ghettos. Before embarking on the public investigation of privatizing a district service, the district's leadership must analyze the probable political repercussions of such a dialogue. The savings in expenditures may not be worth the costs in employee morale or community support.

Most board members are aware that dramatic innovation can create political instability. Should board of education members risk their personal reputations and the stability of the education of students in order to investigate privatizing services? There is no single answer. For that matter, there is no assurance that successfully privatizing one district service will necessarily predict success in privatizing other services in the same district. Research reinforces the experience portrayed in Chapter 1 that the success of privatizing a public service is situational. Success is dependent on the specific circumstances found in the district and the availability of a suitable private contract tailored to the district needs, mixed together with the political climate of the district at the time the decision is made.

The board should avoid preoccupation with its own concerns about privatizing at the expense of forgetting the issues that members of the staff and community bring to the debate. The greater the number of jobs to be impacted by the potential shift to a private company and the greater the staff and community interest, the more formidable will be the board's job of convincing the community of the need for the change.

Open communication is an absolute requirement for success in maximizing community support for important change. Closed session consideration of any policy change, especially when the results may impact district jobs, is certain to exacerbate the conflict, even if such meetings are legal. Such meetings foster suspicion on the part of employees and members of the community. However, no matter how necessary, encouraging community access to the decision-making process will probably not be simple. Working against the intention to have open dialogue may be the self-interest of staff and/or community groups whose position may gain a strong foothold in the community. These expressions can tie up the board in ways described in the vignette that starts this chapter.

Nevertheless, an astute board assures the community that it will conduct an orderly, open process. This will include scheduled, well-publicized, open meetings. Board members can initiate the process of openness by providing for public comment throughout their initial policy deliberation. Once the policy is in place, staff and community will be interested in participating in the design of the process that will be used for examining the alternatives to providing for district staffed functions.

School Administration

A clear articulation of the reasons for considering the transfer of services to the private sector is an important strategy for minimizing the likelihood or intensity of a backlash from staff or community. Further, the potential for failure of the public/private relationship increases dramatically when the transfer is not rooted in logic. The reasoning must be substantial and consistently explained by all district officials even when an authorizing policy is already in place.

The superintendent and his/her staff must have a common understanding of the board's intentions when they translate policy into the action plan that the administration usually has the responsibility to craft. Privatizing is such an incendiary issue that it may not be possible or even preferable for board members to stay totally removed from crossing the line between the policy-making function and the administrative function of working through a process to select a vendor. Some board members will respond to the intense community and staff interest that accompanies this topic by wanting to take an active role in reviewing cost analyses, soliciting bidders, participating in community discussion groups, and even negotiating directly with both vendors and district employee groups. Such involvement may or may not be the style of board members in every district, but it is sure to be a concern that will need to be addressed by the administration. It would be wise to chisel out the respective roles of board and administration for every step in vendor selection during the policy development phase of the privatization process.

Searching for a Partner

It will be the task of the administration to implement the vendor selection process and assure the board and the community that district policy is implemented fairly. Competing vendors will each struggle for maximum attention. Selecting a successful company will make the board, superintendent, and district look good. Choosing the wrong company will create more problems than those that were generated when the district performed the service directly.

Though in some cases vendors will search out the district, districts can take the initiative by placing solicitations for vendors in regional and national papers and trade magazines. Large districts that establish permissive policies for privatizing will attract the major players. Although a small sample list of vendors can be found in Appendix D of this text, a listing of 1,000 public and private companies that serve the education market is available in the *Education Industry Directory: A Resource Guide to the For-Profit Education Industry* (Wagner, 1996). After developing a list of possible companies, the administration can issue its "Request for Proposals" (RFP) or "Invitation to Bid" (ITB), which will be discussed in Chapter 7.

Since the district will likely receive a number of responses to its RFP/ITBs, there will need to be a system for discovering, beyond pricing, which vendor best suits the district's needs. All potential vendors should be required to respond to the same questions at the same level of comprehensiveness in order to fairly compare one proposal with another. Vendors who believe they have a decent opportunity to win a contract will want to be helpful to the district by volunteering information about their capacity, relevant experiences, staying power, staffing, and fees. However, the district must check the truthfulness of references supplied by applicant vendors.

It will fall to the administration to maintain an "arm's length" relationship with all vendors until the final selection or decision not to engage a contractor is made. But the administration should not be surprised to find that vendors will act unilaterally to share with the community written materials about their companies and participate in community information meetings set up without the approval and sometimes the knowledge of the board and administration. However, vendors should be warned directly, when possible, that pursuit of individual board members is beyond the boundary of acceptable behavior. Here again good policy discussions at the beginning of the process can clarify roles and responsibilities of board members and administrators and reduce the chance that some board member or administrator will be enticed by the blandishments of a vendor.

The administration might begin with a clearly spelled out action plan to execute a "due diligence" investigation of a company once one has been selected. A due diligence action plan should identify specific strategies for examining the company, the individuals and/or groups to be involved in the execution of the study, and the time line for recommendations to the board. The process will need to include a careful examination of the company's financial health, operational history, sustainability of promised quality, and experience in other districts. Each of these factors is analyzed with a view to determining the company's capacity to deliver on all contractual obligations within the district's environment. Ample time must be given to this process. In addition, time lines for each part of the action plan should be made public and adhered to as closely as possible. A properly conducted due diligence will cost money. Travel out of the district, phone calls to references, meeting refreshments, consultation with the district's legal and/or financial advisors, duplication of materials, and secretarial assistance are the kinds of expenses for which a due diligence budget should be established. Finally, it is of primary importance to keep the entire community informed about any deviation in the plan or its time line.

Negative responses to privatizing initiatives are quite likely to be put forward by state and national labor unions. Heidi Steffens, NEA's Senior Policy Analyst, says her organization, "remains opposed to private companies running public schools" (McLaughlin, 1996, p. 1). The sting and impact of this national position is likely to be reflected during privatizing discussions at the local district level, since local labor units will usually support positions taken by their national organizations, particularly if total district management is under consideration. Unions may even receive resources from their state and/or national units to mount intensive lobbying activities against privatizing at the local level.

One local district superintendent who was engaged in leading the due diligence process invited representatives from all labor groups and various community organizations to ask their constituents to develop a list of questions that should be investigated in order to determine whether a contract should be signed. This resulted in nearly 1,200 questions. These were merged into a list of over 600 questions, which further consolidated into 46 issues in five categories, which became a template for conducting the due diligence investigation of the company. The board of education, with the help of its own advisory committee, studied these issues and requested the administration to develop proposed contract language that would respond to the issues identified.

The flip side of the due diligence process described above is the vendor's pursuit of information about the district. Every vendor will be anxious to discover all pertinent facts about the district that are relevant to the company's design of a RFP/ITB response so as to assure reasonable profits.

The administration should prepare all the information it deems relevant as part of its proposal request process. In addition, the superintendent and staff should be prepared to invest the time of the district business office and other personnel resources to assist vendors in collecting the information they need for their due diligence. A proposal based upon faulty assumptions will be of no benefit to the district and can result in expensive litigation.

Involving Staff in the Process

The need to improve productivity through cost reduction, the lack of sufficient personnel to provide a quality service, the lack of technical expertise, and/or a requirement for improved management are among the major reasons for contracting out services and programs. These are all rational and appropriate goals for a school board, which carries the community's trust that tax dollars will be spent wisely on behalf of children. But resistance from school district employees is usually the greatest source of political challenge for the board and one of the most important reasons why privatization does not work.

A board of education should not rely on the dictum that favorable results drive out fear. The fear surrounding dramatic change can spiral into uncontrollable dimensions long before results are measured. Further, fear can often find ways to undermine the potential for good results. As one union representative whose board was considering hiring EAI allegedly was told by a leader in the state teachers association, "You have the fate of teachers throughout our country in your hands."

Initially, economic conditions are the paramount concern of educational employee negotiating activities. Higher salaries and increased fringe benefits were and continue to be the primary focus of the negotiating process. But as Herzberg et al. recognized as early as 1959, "Teachers will transcend these monetary concerns after the initial economic thrust (of negotiations). All staff want to be involved in the conduct of the educational enterprise . . . most importantly they want a voice in how district business affects them personally" (p. 6). School district employees, whether in collective bargaining units or not, will insist on a role in the privatization discussion since they will recognize that their welfare will inevitably be impacted.

Educational employees have considerable clout in their communities. Each district employee can have enormous impact on the psychology of district residents by talking to parents, friends, and neighbors. It is consequently easy to understand how board meetings can sometimes develop into raucous, barely controllable events.

The most potent antidote to a strong emotional response is to provide the largest possible involvement of potentially impacted staff in every step of the process. Deborah McGriff notes that the Edison Project solicits as partners only those districts where union leadership will become part of the solution.

SUMMARY

Boards should investigate privatizing when there is evidence that it can be the solution to a real problem. Having a clear purpose for the privatizing initiative will avoid pressures to engage a private company because to do so is in vogue or because such an action emulates the experiences of board members in private industry or because of a demand from influential members of the community. A successful privatizing experience will usually depend upon having very clearly articulated objectives, a careful analysis of the likelihood of a private contractor being better able to achieve these objectives than district staff, and specific methods identified to measure the success of the public/private partnership. Staff will be far less resistant to contracting when they believe they have impacted the process by contributing to the development of board policy and have helped collect and validate the data from the due diligence process. Staff can also be consulted for the development of specifications for the RFP/ITB.

Every small and large step in the move toward privatization will gain credibility and the final result will have greater acceptance if those affected are active participants in shaping the results.

CHAPTER 6

The Politics of Privatization

Three agitated parents, with their preschool age children in tow, asked the receptionist to see the superintendent immediately. During the ensuing discussion, the parents admitted that they lived in a neighboring district, but they were adamant that the board's consideration of privatizing was yet another example, together with outcomes based education, of big government trying to control the lives of parents and children. Though admittedly not residents of the district, they portrayed themselves as representatives of district residents who were members of the Lyndon LaRouche organization. Their request to distribute anti-privatizing, pro-LaRouche materials on school grounds was immediately denied. These parents invited the superintendent to a protest meeting the next evening. Except for a handful of local LaRouche supporters and a couple of excitable students, the rally drew few participants. Further, the superintendent was informed that four bus loads of protesters from three Midwestern states would be coming to the district the following week to picket against privatizing. In response to this threat of outsiders intent on creating some havoc, the district was forced to hire a private property protection company to augment its staff and the small local police department so as to secure district facilities and the learning processes within them. The outside protesters never materialized and the extra expense of hiring the guards then became a topic of intense public debate at the subsequent board meeting.

INTRODUCTION

School governance is the implementation of a political process. *Webster's New Collegiate Dictionary* defines "politics" as being concerned with "the making as distinguished from the administration of government policy." In a democracy, politics is the process whereby

81

citizens, working through their elected officials, make policy decisions about how government should operate.

The universal imperatives of effective school district governance—broad public participation in important policy decisions and widespread and accurate information regularly distributed to all citizens—are the foundation for dealing with all hotly contested issues, including privatization initiatives. Therefore, the best protection against the small or large community turmoil that may accompany a privatization discussion is to have in place an ongoing system of public information and community involvement.

But no board of education should initiate a public discussion about contracting any function without first deciding whether the political, economic, and social consequences of a decision to privatize will result in stronger, weaker, or undiminished support for the schools on the part of district residents.

THE SOCIAL COST OF POLITICAL TURMOIL

This chapter, in fact the concept of this book, began from an experience of almost total community turmoil as a school district considered whether to privatize most district operations, instructional and non-instructional. The social cost of this turmoil was a loss of faith by parents, educators, and the community at large in their educational system and a breakdown of trust in the system's policymakers.

The calculus of controversy—that is, the relationship between the size of the community, the size of the privatization initiative, and the level of controversy that is likely to result—cannot be predicted. It may be logical to assume that the smaller the initiative, the less controversy that is likely to ensue, but that is no certainty. The attempt of the Wilkinsburg, Pennsylvania School District to contract out the operation of just one school became a nationally publicized dispute.

In one district, a proposed switch from a district-run transportation system to a contracted system could result in a few contentious board meetings and then a return to normalcy. In another community, the same proposal could lead to petitions for school board recall, furiously contested school board elections, and neighbor pitted against neighbor in a raucous community debate.

Today almost any privatization initiative is likely to create some community controversy. If district employees affected by the proposal are members of a bargaining unit, especially one represented by the National Education Association (NEA) and, to a slightly lesser extent, the American Federation of Teachers, the community debate is a virtual certainty. In fact, the NEA (1995a) has published a 59-page guide to its members describing how to organize to oppose any privatization effort.

This book has not argued for or against privatization. Earlier chapters have shown that privatization of government functions is a growing phenomenon. There are good arguments, based on economics and program delivery, for privatizing services in some school districts. There are good arguments, based on economics and social policy, against privatizing. The rest of this chapter will be devoted to a discussion of techniques for managing community debate, the politics of privatizing, if a school district decides that a contracting initiative should enter the discussion stage.

THE POLITICAL CONTEXT

Successfully privatizing school district programs or services will require the reconciliation of public, employees, and special interests. These interests can emerge from within the district or be imported from outside the district. The district's choice of strategy for making a change can also fundamentally affect the community discussion.

Public opinion can resemble a chameleon. Citizens increasingly demand the lowest possible tax rate yet insist that schools provide a high quality education for all students. However, citizen focus on cost effectiveness is too easily forgotten in a debate that causes all sides to take strong, extreme, and unyielding positions about privatizing. Once the investigation of contracting begins, the state and national organizations to which school employees belong (e.g., AFSCME, NEA, AFT, etc.) frequently respond with alarm. To compound the difficulty, unaffected groups sometimes seize upon the political upheaval to move forward their unrelated political agenda. As illustrated at the beginning of the chapter, the result can be an infusion of outside individuals and organizations who become players in the drama. The tactics of any and all of these groups often include the vilification of the district's leadership. Moving toward a privatization decision in some communities can result in a searing emotional experience for board members and administrators.

The strategy for managing the political process of decision making should be undertaken with this possibility in mind.

If a school board does not have credibility with the general population before it begins to debate privatizing issues, it will unlikely be able to respond effectively to pressure tactics. It will consequently have great difficulty in making the tough decisions that are required over time to implement its privatizing initiatives. School board members who are considering a major policy change will want to assess the current state of their relationships with the public and the quality of the district's public information program before proceeding. If serious deficiencies can be identified in either of these areas, a privatization initiative may not be timely, no matter how much sense it might make in economic terms. Politically healthy school districts appear to provide the best environments in which to nurture the new relationships that come from privatizing. Board members in successful districts have a broad based and supportive constituency, a necessity to withstand the withering pressure that often accompanies privatizing actions.

CONFLICT MANAGEMENT

The Process

The politics of privatizing are complicated, but not unmanageable. An essential prerequisite for a rational decision-making process is a complete understanding of the interests of all players and a carefully conceived plan for organizing the political process to reach a broadly supported decision. The district must remember that simply agreeing to privatize is not enough. The innovation will require the goodwill necessary to buy enough time to show results. This ambitious goal can be achieved only if all parties feel they have been given adequate attention during deliberations on the issue. A high-profile consideration of the privatization alternative will be difficult and usually messy, but the debate will be infinitely more difficult and considerably more untidy for a much longer period of time if a truly representative process isn't used.

To maintain control of the process, which is one of the main goals of a well-designed political strategy, the board should develop a study plan once the possibility of privatization elicits enough interest to warrant consideration. Good planning will increase the chance that discussions will be issue-focused rather than heated and emotional debates.

Everyone and anyone who will be impacted by the privatizing decision, and anyone who knows someone who will be impacted, can be expected to want to influence the privatizing decision. Politically astute district leadership will use a flexible plan that attempts to predict, monitor, and manage the events of the planning process. Managing a process is not synonymous with manipulating it. The goal of managing is the assurance of a complete and thorough investigation. The goal of manipulation is to shape the decision.

A viable political process will have as a minimum the following elements:

- Identification and involvement of the organized stakeholders as well as other community groups that will support a rational investigation. It is important to recognize students as an interested group. They will be heard from, one way or the other.
- A strategy for debate and discussion that will assure the voicing of all existing and evolving points of view in a safe and rational environment. The structure, venue, and pacing of the debate will need to be planned.

There is no limit to the techniques through which an effective and representative study process can be carried out. The final decision about how to assure a thoughtful and broadly representative deliberation will depend on many factors: the personal style and temperament of board members and the superintendent; the presence or absence of group process skills in the staff and in the community; community traditions in discussing difficult issues; and other factors. As long as the process is fair, objective, rational, and public, almost any approach might be chosen. Some of the more common decision-making processes used by school districts are described below.

All processes begin with an announcement by the board of education of its interest in considering a policy regarding contracting and the adoption of policies that support investigation of privatization opportunities. With policies in place and a clear purpose for considering a contracting initiative identified, the district can then move to a defined process for considering a concrete proposal to privatize.

(1) *Board Hearings:* The board of education states its intention to hold hearings on the possibility of contracting with a private firm. Dates and locations, and rules and procedures for the conduct of these meetings are widely disseminated. Information about the date and location of the board meeting at which the final decision will be made is also announced.

(2) *Community Study Group:* The board announces its intention to use a study group consisting of representatives from community groups to consider the possibility of contracting. The board also indicates whether it will appoint a person nominated by each identified group or appoint a person from each group of its own choosing. Stakeholders who have no organized group, such as non-parents, would be selected by the board. The board also indicates how committee leadership will be selected. Options include having an administrator skilled in group process chair the group, having the board appoint a widely respected and disinterested citizen to chair the group, or allowing the group, when formed, to select its own leader. A clearly written mission is provided by the board to the study committee. An information conduit to the board should be established at the outset. Either an administrator or a board member who can monitor the work of the study committee toward completion of the mission should be an ex-officio committee member.

(3) *Focus Group Meetings:* Community groups are identified by some common denominator. For example, one group may consist only of parents, another of senior citizens, a third of business leaders in the community, etc. A carefully designed protocol is used to question group members regarding their feelings about the proposed course of action. A disinterested observer records observations regarding the proposal from each of the groups. A summary of reactions of the various groups is presented to the board of education before it makes a final decision. There is no limit to the number and kind of groups that would be interviewed. At least one group consisting of employees would be an absolute requirement.

Each of these approaches has its advantages and disadvantages. If the board itself runs the hearings, it can be accused of listening for what it wants to hear. "Representative" community groups are always difficult to appoint. If the community organization selects its own representative for the committee, there is no assurance that the board will get a person who is both fair and open to new ideas. If the board picks the group's representative, it can be accused of "stacking" the committee to get the decision it wants. Focus group interviews require some technical knowledge on the part of the person designing the interview protocol and restraint on the part of the interviewer. Participants in the groups must be guided to respond to the questions under consideration without drifting into extraneous matters. No matter how skillful the leader of focus groups, challenges are possible as to the accuracy of the leader's conclusions about what the group actually said.

The only certainty in working for a decision that will be widely supported is the need for some community-based deliberative process. Without such resident involvement subsequent months or years of continued opposition can be expected once a contracting decision is made.

The Players

Alignments among the key stakeholders—school board members, business leaders, clergy, district employees, parents, students, and others—can be fluid, shifting unpredictably depending upon the issues that arise at each stage of the debate. In part, this lack of constancy of view is a result of the different hats worn by residents. The authors have led school organizations where school employees whose paychecks would benefit from a school tax increase were willing to campaign against the ballot proposal because it would raise their own property tax. In another situation, teachers and school principals aligned against a school tax renewal because their unions advocated that such support would aide the board's privatizing effort.

Some group dynamics can be anticipated; some cannot. The better organized a group, whether an employee or community organization, the more likely its members will put forward a common and consistent position. The better funded the group, the greater the potential for that group to measurably influence other stakeholders through the expenditure of human and financial resources. Pinckney School District teachers effectively organized afternoon teas to "inform" parents about their opposition to privatizing, and the teachers union financed the printing of signs opposing the privatizing effort. These signs appeared in a very large number of front yards along the major arteries of the district.

If citizens lack information about the governing board's position on a controversial issue, it is highly probable that they will adopt the position to which they have been exposed, especially if exposed repeatedly from a variety of sources.

The following section presents a brief overview of some of the more prominent community stakeholder groups that will need to be involved in planning the district's study strategy and participating in the process.

The Board of Education

A good community discussion process begins with the board of education giving clearly articulated reasons for proposing the privatization solution. The board and administration need to be honest, first with themselves and then with the community, about the fundamental interests that drive the initiative. They should be able to answer the following questions for the community:

- Is the district trying to save money? Does it know how much it is likely to save?
- Is the district trying to provide a new service, like foreign language instruction?
- Has it tried alternative solutions that might not so drastically affect district employees, such as setting up a cooperative program with a neighboring district or districts?
- Does the current program suffer from poor quality? What steps have been taken to improve quality before turning to privatization?
- If none of the district's remediation strategies were successful, what is there about the proposed contracting solution that offers a better likelihood that the board will achieve its goals of higher quality, lower cost, or both?
- *What are the risks involved in taking this step?*

The board should also be honest regarding the likely impact of contracting on employees. If a contract to operate a school is written with the Edison Project, the consequences for staff may be mild since Edison will not come into a district without the overt support of the teachers and their union, if one exists. Only those teachers who volunteer to teach in an Edison school will be assigned there (McGriff, 1995). However, in the Wilkinsburg, Pennsylvania, contract with Alternative Public Schools the board gave the company authority to replace teachers and hire its own staff. As a consequence of its action in taking over the district's Turner

School, fifteen teachers were laid off and nine were reassigned (*New York Times*, August 30, 1995). Later the Pennsylvania courts reinstated these teachers with back pay. If a board of education judges such a precedent-breaking move essential, it has a right, perhaps an obligation, to make such a decision, but it should publicly acknowledge such a result at the outset. Citizens need to be aware of such significant consequences if they are expected to support the board through whatever labor reactions are forthcoming.

Similar issues arise when contracting support services. Will the board protect the employment rights of its current workers if it contracts for functions such as transportation or food services? To what extent?

Once all relevant data, including known or anticipated consequences, are presented to the public, the function of the ensuing community study/discussion is to confirm the board's conclusions and data. At this stage the board may be offered other alternatives by employee groups and by the community. When starting the final deliberations about contracting, board members and executive administrators are well advised to admit any hardship such a move might bring to loyal and hardworking employees. A plan, at least a preliminary plan, to ease the burden on local workers if a contract is consummated shows both employees and community that the board's goal is not to hurt employees, but to become more cost effective/efficient so as to target more dollars toward instruction. Both the Wilkinsburg, Pennsylvania, and the Pinckney, Michigan, investigations of privatization came during or after difficult labor negotiations. Unintended or not, this sequence of events suggests to disinterested parties that the respective boards of education were attempting to achieve through privatization what they could not obtain by collective bargaining. Board members should not be surprised if the ensuing discussion becomes bitterly acrimonious.

Administrators

It is critically important to share the design of a privatization study with district administrators. If building level administrators are knowledgeable about the purposes of the study and the process that will be used, they can be helpful in calming staff and community. If administrators are uninformed or misinformed about the district's study plans, they can become equally threatened and possibly compound the confusion as they interact with staff and the public.

When the board's outsourcing goal is to improve the management of a district function, the administrator whose job is on the line may have mixed feelings of loyalty to the district and/or the superintendent. If the program administrator can be assured that he or she will be reassigned within the district or that every effort will be made to have a contractor employ this individual, public or covert opposition to the contracting initiative by this individual can be minimized.

Staff

Certainly for employees, many of whom may be district residents, the possibility that the district will move to privatizing one or more district services is a traumatic event. Emotions can run high. Board members may quickly become the targets of anger and invective, similar to the Hartford, Connecticut, and Wilkinsburg, Pennsylvania, experiences, which led to bitterly fought board elections over this one issue. Community turmoil can happen well before a rational discussion ever gets initiated unless the board plans strategically to manage the discussion process once the idea of privatization has enough support on the board to initiate a deliberative process.

The organizations that represent employees are a major force for both stimulating and resisting change. It is almost always the organization's leadership that articulates the political position of the group. As noted earlier, pressure on local employee union leadership from regional, state, and sometimes national organizations will usually be intense enough to shape the position of the local union. The ability of a school board to move ahead in the face of strong employee opposition will depend on the board's ability to build a constituency for change among other community stakeholders.

The predictably strong employee opposition to the privatizing of one of the district's functions will be contagious, affecting all employee groups, even if the district does not contemplate privatizing additional services. It will be difficult to prevent the fear of outsourcing from becoming a general alarm sometimes expressed as "the foot in the door syndrome." This contagion can result in the pooling of human and financial resources by unaffected employee groups.

Parents

Many of America's approximately 15,500 school districts are assisted and supported by organizations of parents and teachers that focus on the quality of education within their local school. These affiliations range from a largely unstructured group of parents to a well-organized PTA/PTO accustomed to exercising a strong influence over who gets to be the next board member, principal, and even superintendent. If a well-organized group of parents exists within the district, the membership will be an organizational target for propaganda of both anti-privatizing and pro-privatizing forces. The board and administration's working relationship with the leadership of the local school PTA/PTO will be important in generating unbiased consideration of such a contentious issue.

The Business Community

The business perspective, in some communities articulated by a chamber of commerce, will usually have a bias in favor of privatizing. However, the opinions of individual business leaders will be highly dependent on their own situation. A local hardware store owner will want to know if the companies being considered for a facilities management contract will continue to buy products from his corner store. The local heating contractor will ask whether he can bid on the heating and air-conditioning work if the district signs a contract with a private company. These are understandable questions that are obviously driven by concern about economic security, the same concerns that motivate opposition from district employees.

The smaller the community, the more personally and widely felt are the answers. Everyone might know and even buy from the corner gas station owner who will no longer provide the fuel for the district's buses if a contractor with huge buying power gets the transportation contract. Profit generated by the district's fuel purchases might be the difference between staying in business or closing the only gas station in town. A board of education should carefully review community dynamics and perhaps informally test out business opinion before initiating a public study.

Clergy

In many of America's districts, large and small, the clergy have significant influence on the thinking of the district's constituency. Clergy who choose to speak from the pulpit about education issues may only be reflecting the views of a few of their congregation. School district leadership can take advantage of the significant interest of clergy in the community's affairs by organizing these influential and important community leaders into discussion groups around the major issues before the district. Obviously, members of the clergy will form their own position on such matters, but a sound political strategy will make certain that they have all the facts before they speak to their congregations. The school district provides a common bond among the many denominations within most communities. It is probable that the district's clergy have seldom met together to discuss any issue, unless the district has initiated and facilitated such meetings. Clergy can and will assist in helping the community focus on the substance and not the emotion of the issue if they understand the facts of the situation. However, religious leaders also respond to the needs of their constituency and can be persuasive against an issue as well. Here is another group that ought to be probed very early in the process. Religious leaders can give district officials an excellent window on current views within the community.

Elected Officials

Other than board members, or in those cases where municipal and/or regional politicians have direct school district policy control, elected local and state officials who represent the district will probably not want to be involved in the discussion about privatizing school district functions. The smaller the politician's voting constituency, the more local the politician, the less likely he or she will initially take a position on privatizing. The initial debate is usually viewed as a "no win" proposition for a local politician's career. But unless the district's political plan considers how to keep these officials informed, it may lose their neutrality, especially if the board is considering an unpopular vote. School leadership must accept the reality that a politician's public statements may sometimes have more to do with vote solicitation than principled commitment.

Media

Studies have shown that most non-parents view newspapers as their primary source of information about schools. In smaller districts, print media may be the single most potent force for shaping opinions about the district's programs and operations. Local newspapers consistently write about local district events and news. If the issue is sufficiently newsworthy, such as Pinckney's consideration of EAI as its education management organization, media attention from outside the community can be significant. Though admittedly not a typical situation, the Pinckney district experienced calls and visits from regional, state, and even national print and visual media. There were days, sometimes weeks, when most of the administration's time was spent responding to these media interests. It can be a pretty energizing experience for a school board member to be interviewed by *USA Today*, *Newsweek*, or *Time* magazine. If the excitement escalates and all are enjoying their fifteen minutes of fame talking to the media, the district can run the risk of sending multiple, often conflicting, messages to the public. When this happens, credibility is almost certain to be lost. Only the creation of a district public information plan, if one doesn't already exist, can avoid serious damage to the district's perceived integrity.

The goal of an effective school district information plan is to provide reliable data directly to citizens before the media publicizes details of the discussion, though admittedly this can be a challenging task. The plan should also disaggregate the various constituencies in the community and decide how each of these constituencies will be provided reliable information on a continuing basis and who will provide it. If internal expertise is not available to develop and/or execute such a plan, professional help should be sought. Public relations firms are a good example of private companies that provide services for a limited purpose and short time horizon, which may not economically be provided internally in the district. This is outsourcing at its best.

Students

It has already been noted that students are an interest group. They will find a way to be heard. Planning for students to receive factual information about any change in their environment will reduce the possibility that they will use the debate as an excuse for an active protest. All staff who interact with students must be reminded, sometimes repeatedly, against giving one-sided views about the contracting discussion and its substance. From a positive point of view, the community's effort to reach a decision about contracting provides a significant opportunity for students to learn about how the democratic process operates in resolving difficult issues. Staff should be encouraged to integrate the subject into classroom activities at appropriate grade levels.

Special Groups

Of course each district will have also its own special groups (senior citizens, athletic boosters, Rotary members, etc.) which, because of their influence on public opinion, will need to be part of the discussion process, not just observers of the results of the discussion. Decisions will have to be made at the very beginning of the process about whether any groups from outside the community will be involved in the debate in any way and how their access to the process should or can be circumscribed if they are not involved.

COMMUNITY REACTIONS

The "total quality" movement in the private sector begins by answering the question, "Who is our customer?" This is a far easier task for entrepreneurs than for educators. Is the district's customer the student? The companies and corporations that ultimately hire the graduating student? Are parents, who trust educators to protect and nurture their prize possession, the customers? Certainly all the taxpayers who fund the district, whether or not they have a direct relationship to schools and children, cannot be ignored when seeking to identify the "customer." At least from one perspective all of these constituencies can be thought of as customers. It is this diffusion of accountability that led Burt Nanus, a leading theoretician of organizational leadership in the private sector, to conclude that "a public sector organization is responsive to a much wider array of influences and interests than that of a private corporation, making the task of scoping a vision for such an agency much more complicated" (Nanus, 1995, p.195).

The difficulty of managing a public organization is further complicated in that any individual resident may represent several different kinds of customers simultaneously. The CEO of a district tax paying company (the business customer) may also have children in the district's schools (the parent customer). This person might also be on the school board. Each of these roles requires its own perspective. These perspectives can sometimes be overlapping, sometimes contradictory. Every district resident must be considered a stockholder who will be impacted by the eventual outcome of the privatizing debate, and information about the issue needs to be presented to each person from the appropriate frame of reference if possible.

Ideologues on all sides of the privatizing issue prefer the heat generated by an investigation rather than the light a study might bring, but a good decision-making process forces the players to focus on facts. The words "all sides" are used since third parties, often from outside the district, can enter the debate with agendas far different from those of any of the district's major players, the board, administration, employees, and parents. Opponents of "outcomes based education," " critical thinking," "self-esteem" and other common topics of public discord often see any public controversy as a promising opportunity to build alliances with other disaffected groups and individuals. Only thoughtfully planned strategies for managing the discussion can keep such undesired events from happening. Specific decisions must be made at the outset of the discussion process as to how the opinions of individuals and groups from outside the district will be acknowledged.

CREATING NEW POSSIBILITIES

School boards expecting private companies to become the vehicle for restoring their trustworthiness or political capital will have no more success than those married couples who decide to have a child as a means of saving their conflicted marriages. Adding more players can complicate the situation and produce more problems around which the parties can polarize. School boards that have studied a problem carefully and dispassionately and openly shared their findings with the community have usually been able to bring about a transition to a new way of doing business and providing quality education.

A library of books has been written about how to bring about institutional change. Many of these volumes have been devoted to the question of how to make changes in public education. A major question, for which there is no universal answer, centers on whether it is better to make changes in small increments, thereby allowing people to become accustomed to the change, or whether it is better to impose "breakthrough" changes in one broad sweep, thereby obviating the opportunity for opponents of the change to crush it while it still does not represent the standard way of operating. Each board of education and administrative team will have to decide this question. However, in the absence of a crisis situation, there is good reason to believe that small, pilot changes provide more compelling evidence of the success of a change in a particular school district than any argument that insists that what has worked elsewhere is certain to work in the subject district and therefore sweeping change is implemented. Concrete results achieved within the district are the best argument to convince what might be, or become, a skeptical public.

SUMMARY

Given the anti-tax sentiment that pervades the country, school boards seem to have no alternative but to try innovative approaches that promise more results for the same or less money. This lack of resources has led to the use of private companies to provide support services and, in a few cases, the employment of companies to improve the achievement of one or more district schools. But as the *New York Times* has noted, "when they [such companies] have to rely on the support and cooperation of school boards that failed in the past under pressure from politics, unions and other interests" it is questionable whether private entrepreneurs can succeed in environments which are not culturally and therefore politically aligned to the privatizing strategies (*New York Times,* March 1, 1996). It is the task of the school board and executive administrators to design a process for deliberating a privatizing decision that will involve all stakeholders and thereby create the necessary political alignment.

For example, EAI proposed to the Hartford, Connecticut, board that budget expenditures be reduced by eliminating 220 teachers and 100 other employees. "The proposal was a political disaster, loudly protested by teachers who had claimed all along that the company's plan was to save costs by substituting computers for teachers" (*New York Times,* March 11, 1996). It would seem clear that the Hartford board members did not have a political constituency that would step forward and assist them in examining the merits of an issue rather than react to the pressure from a vested group.

Frances E. Winslow (1991) has noted that "All successful political plans for privatization have the voter as their base. Support or dissent starts with those who have the power of the vote" (p. 137). It is possible to know everything about the need to privatize one or more functions of a school district and still be unsuccessful. Unless the public is convinced a privatization initiative will have positive economic consequences for the district and the citizens both in the short and long term, the effort will

Carefully Plan and Organize. Look down the entire road when evaluating productivity levels and the need to privatize. Begin with enabling board policy, and try to strategize each step and identify each of the players. Create a climate of problem solving that does not assess blame or cite one group for failure.

Establish Consensus through Coalition Building. Invite a diverse coalition to investigate the district's productivity levels and other needs that may lead to privatizing. Involve in the consensus building activities interested people who represent a full range of perspectives and politics—business leaders, parents, teachers, higher education representatives, community leaders, students, and potentially affected employee groups.

Be Prepared to Change. Change the membership and structure of advisory groups as their group's missions and strategies change. Consider establishing more than one advisory group with distinctly different missions. Avoid allowing one interest group, perspective, or viewpoint to dominate the group membership.

Keep the Discussions Broadly Based. Initially, focus debate and investigations on the broad productivity needs of the district. Refrain from discussing specific solutions until later. Avoid scapegoating any one group for problems within the district by staying issue-oriented. Don't frighten staff unnecessarily.

Involve the Media. Engage the media in support of the solution by including them as important partners. Organize opportunities for the media to have access to information, opinion leaders, and onsite visits.

Don't Promise a Miracle. Be realistic about the potential benefits of outsourcing district activities or services. Be realistic in promising benefits.

Learn First. Encourage coalition members to read, visit, and learn about issues, theories, practice, and policy before embarking on the pursuit of a specific solution involving privatizing. Other solutions internal and cooperative may be more suitable.

Tailor the Solutions. Contracting with private entities is not a patented process. Learn from the progress and mistakes of other districts, within and outside the state. But do not engage in privatizing simply because it has been found suitable for a neighboring district.

Consensus—Maybe! Recognize that group consensus is optimal, but not always possible. Don't let negative members generate the dominant atmosphere.

Stay in Charge. Private companies may suggest time lines, strategies, and contract terms that transfer responsibility for managing the process and even ultimate control of the service from the school board to the company board. Enter contract negotiations with a firm list of terms that are best suited to the district and that maintain the district as final decision maker.

Make a Situational Decision. Match the specific needs of the educational community to the strategies employed to improve productivity. Include the social cost of privatizing when weighing the factors. Every community is different, and each needs to establish its own priorities.

Figure 6.1. *Managing the Political Process: A Telescopic View.*

be a failure. It is the responsibility of leadership to manage a political process that permits the case to be made effectively to the voters. The authors hope Figure 6.1 will be of assistance in that effort.

CHAPTER 7

Assuring an Effective Contract

The district had lost several ballot attempts to raise property taxes to support the schools. A team of board candidates had decided that more money wasn't what was needed. Rather, the district had to use the money it had more wisely. One member of the team had heard a speaker on the subject of using private companies to provide services traditionally supplied by government workers and convinced the other team members that privatization was the "magic bullet" to solve many of the district's financial problems. The team was elected.

They immediately invited a speaker on privatization to present at a board meeting. Anxious employees packed the meeting. He assured the board that privatization would provide virtually all services less expensively and more effectively. The board immediately declared themselves in favor of privatization.

Legal costs alone subsequently wiped out and exceeded first year savings that were achieved when the school busing function was privatized later that year. But the company bought new, more reliable buses, resulting in a significant improvement in on-time pickups. The outcome was a dramatic decrease in parent complaints to the central office. Starting in the second year projected savings were realized.

INTRODUCTION

Education, including training and development programs for private businesses, is a 600 billion dollar industry nationwide, with 307.5 billion spent on kindergarten through twelfth grade schooling and 30 billion dollars on preschool education. Education consumes 8.9% of the gross domestic product. Health care is the only industry consuming more

99

dollars than education (Wagner, 1996). Given the worldwide political climate described earlier, it is no surprise that private industry looks enthusiastically on public education as a ripe market.

Schools currently spend about 15 billion dollars on educational products like textbooks, computers, and software. Reliable figures on the dollar volume of contracts with private companies for programs such as food service, school transportation, maintenance and operations, and other support services are not available because of the rapidly changing environment (Figure 7.1). Studies of each of these ancillary services show that the dollar volume is growing. Beales, an advocate of privatization, has suggested that "private contractors provide roughly 30% of bus service and 10% of custodial and maintenance services and operate at least 7% of school cafeterias" (Beales, 1994, p. 2). *School Bus Fleet* puts the figure for school bus transportation at 28% (January, 1994).

Agreements with companies to manage the instructional programs of one or more schools are increasing though they are still a very small proportion of the total number of contracts with private vendors. A study conducted in the winter of 1993 by the Illinois Education Association of 850 school districts with a return rate of slightly over 40% (about 340 districts) found that 33% contracted for transportation services, 20% for food services and 11% for custodial and maintenance services (NEA, 1995a). A study of Pennsylvania school districts in 1985–86 found that

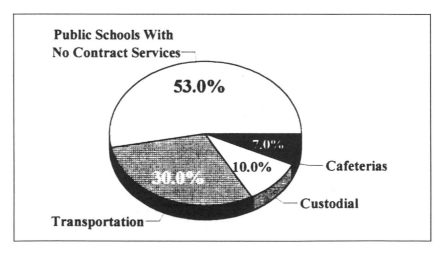

Figure 7.1. Private Contractors Provide Contract Services for Only a Small Segment of the Public School Sector. (Of all public schools, contract services are used by 30% for transportation, 10% for custodial services, and 7% for food services. Beales, 1994)

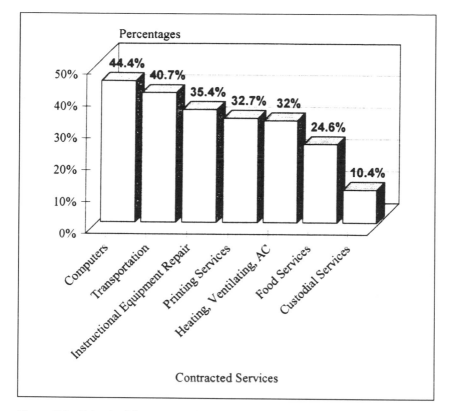

Figure 7.2. *Privatized Services Used by 66% of 300 Districts Surveyed by the Journal* American School & University *in 1993.*

about two thirds of the districts contracted bus service. By 1987–88 that figure had risen to 75% (NEA, 1995a). One study estimates that "for profit companies take in $30 billion" of the over $300 billion the United States spends each year on preschool to high school education (*New York Times*, May 30, 1996).

Paul Abramson (1993), on behalf of *American School and University* magazine, identified the number of school districts using contracted services as of that date (Figure 7.2). Some of his findings are summarized in Table 7.1. An advantage of his study was a report of findings by school district size as well as the summary statistics included in Table 7.1. However, the author gave no statistical information regarding the number of school districts polled or the rate of response, so questions about the accuracy of the information may be raised. His study shows a higher rate of contracted transportation than other studies. It cannot be

Table 7.1. *Percentage of School Districts Using Contracted Services.*

Type of Service	Districts Using
Transportation (busing)	40.7%
Food service	24.6%
Custodial	10.4%
Maintenance	11.1%
Computer servicing	44.4%
Instructional equipment repair	35.4%
Printing	32.7%
Mechanical system maintenance	32.0%

determined whether his data are more accurate. Nevertheless the report is suggestive of the current frequency of privatizing in local school districts. The data are likely changing every day anyway.

It seems inevitable that school districts will be increasingly likely to consider writing a contract with an individual or a company for service. Doyle (1994), Odden (1996), and others have noted that education financing is likely to remain static or decline, in the near future at least. Doing more, or at least better, with less will be an imperative, not a slogan. Opinion polls show that the public wants better public education. The devolution of entitlement programs to states, along with their own growing costs for health care, prisons, and other human services, will mean fewer dollars for education. Education will no longer be insulated from comparisons regarding cost effectiveness or service quality (Pirie, 1988, p. 18). Contracting will become a more significant option than ever before. Badly written contracts can result in embarrassment, costly revisions and additions, poor service, and other highly undesirable consequences. Perhaps the only error worse than not considering contracting for any program or service, a highly unlikely outcome given the likely financial future of public education, is writing a bad contract.

ISSUES IN CONTRACTING

Legal Issues

Though the following sections of this chapter are designed to assist school officials in the task of reaching a contract that will achieve the defined purposes of the district, it cannot be forgotten that a written contract is a legal document. It is prudent practice for any school district to develop all its contracts with the assistance of a competent attorney; legal assistance would be even more necessary for a contract that breaks new ground and could engender a high-profile community controversy.

It is a well-established principle of law that boards of education have only those powers as are expressly conferred upon them. Studies by the Wisconsin Association of School Boards and the American Association of Educators in Private Practice show that some states give "broad" powers to contract for teaching or administrative services while others "grant enumerated powers or authority for specific instructional programs" (National School Boards Association, 1995a, p. 6). In the state of Michigan, the meaning of "expressly conferred" is usually limited to actions that are "necessary to the program of study" (51 Mich. App. 305, 1974). In California it is not legally permissible to contract for management/supervisory services (Lieberman, 1995, p. 2). Before a lot of administrative time is spent on comparative cost analysis, the district should seek legal advice as to the limits of its ability to contract for services and the legal obligations imposed both on boards and vendors if contracting is permitted. In Michigan the superintendent must be an employee of the district, not of a contractor.

Since contracting for instructional services, especially comprehensive services to manage total building or district operations, is a relatively new phenomenon, statutes on point and case law can be expected to be particularly thin. Unless there is clear legal authority for the district to move ahead, clarification of the board's authority should be sought.

If it becomes clear that contracting with a private vendor is legal under state law, then specific legal issues must be confronted. Employment relationships may be the most critical of these secondary issues to clarify.

Some of the more important questions to be answered include the following:

- Who is the employer of record, the school district or the contractor?
- If faculty and support staff are district employees, is the district or contractor responsible for all salary, benefit, and retirement costs?
- What are the rights of a contractor to discipline a tenured

faculty member who fails to perform according to the contractor's directions or specifications? What authority does the contractor have over other staff who remain employees of the district?

- What is the application of legal obligations of the board of education relative to approving bids, filing state reports, handling public money, and other fiduciary responsibilities when working with a contractor who is to be given responsibility for all operations of a building or district?
- Is there legal authority for a private contractor to keep as profit or its fee any and all unexpended money left in the general fund?
- What are the obligations of a private vendor to disclose how funds were expended and what profits were made?

There is still another level of legal issues too comprehensive to summarize here that should also be investigated before any contract with a vendor is considered. These are legal issues that deal with personnel issues such as the rights of handicapped persons, employee rights to review personnel records, civil rights protections, and due process procedures. (See Appendix B for a more comprehensive list of legal issues that should be considered by the school district and Appendix C for a suggestive list of contractual items to be negotiated.) Obviously no move toward contracting should be made without the professional advice of an attorney knowledgeable in school law.

GENERAL PRINCIPLES OF CONTRACTING

Clear Purpose

The first question the district must decide is the reason or reasons it wishes to contract for a service. Hopefully the justification derives from topics discussed in the previous chapters: high costs, poor service quality, lack of financing to acquire human and technological resources to improve productivity, or other issues related to the mission of the district. The literature is not without examples of government officials who appeared to move toward hiring a private company to provide a service in retaliation against a public employee union with which a difficult negotiation had taken place or which had precipitated a strike or other job action. Experienced government officials realize that negative motivations for actions usually result in bad policy or practice. It is too easy to be "hoisted by one's own petard."

Knowing whether the district is seeking lower costs, better service, or both is critical in designing the details of the invitation to bid (ITB) or request for proposals (RFP) from potential bidders. This information is also critically important in establishing standards and performance measures for which vendors will be held accountable. The ITB process is usually used when detailed contract specifications are possible. Awards for ITBs are usually based on lowest price bids (Rehfuss, 1989). RFPs allow for more flexibility in selection criteria because price becomes only one feature of a successful service. In some states there may be a legally required intermixture of contracting with a service provider and bidding for capital equipment that will be owned by the school district but used by the contractor.

Specific Measures of Performance

The Report of the President's Commission on Privatization (1987) identified several important principles that should be kept in mind by those contemplating entering a contract with a private vendor. "Contracting is likely to be most successful when the terms and measurements of service delivery are clear and closely defined, when several firms have the capacity to perform the contract, when large capital investments don't get made, and contract renewal is frequent" (p. 244).

Ironically it might be easier to set standards for a contractor to meet in improving reading scores than to employ a company to clean a building, since the desired standards of reading accomplishment may be easier to measure through standardized scores than the level of cleanliness of a lavatory. Nevertheless, service contracts that are focused on clearly determined and easily measured standards are far less likely to end up in dispute or, worse, litigation, than contracts that deal with hard to measure or unpredictable human behavior. Writing a contract to raise student reading scores on the fourth grade state assessment test may at first glance seem easy, but such a contract could become subject to the law of unintended consequences; for example, a larger proportion of students recommended for retention in the third grade the year a contract is up for renewal.

Seeking a Competitive Environment

Deciding to privatize a function, especially a function for which a number of viable bidders is not available, may be inadvisable. Dropping a service formerly provided by government employees in favor of a private vendor is frequently a community trauma. To consider only one private company to replace government employees may simply substitute one form of monopoly for another and hardly justify the emotional turmoil that will be experienced by employees and their friends and relatives in the community. Though the initial contract with a company may seem to promise cost efficiencies or quality improvements, the government agency can be caught in a bind when the contract comes up for renewal. It could now face paying whatever rate the company bids or go back into performing the service with its own employees. Obviously such a step could prove highly embarrassing at best. Contracting with a private company to manage a school or schools doesn't usually present the same number of problems since the company usually uses the district's teachers.

Even before starting the formal bidding process, it is wise to do some preliminary investigation of private firms that will be interested in doing business in the district in order to have a realistic estimate of the price that will be required to employ a competent vendor. The worst of all worlds for government officials is to engage in a painful political process of talking about privatizing and then find either that there are no interested companies or that the cost of privatizing the service will be more expensive than providing the service with government employees.

Avoiding Conflicts of Interest

If it appears that there will be real competition to provide a service, the district can then deal with several policy issues before beginning to define the details of a bid or create a contract. Potential conflict of interest issues are at the top of the list of such policy matters.

If shortly after leaving the school district a key district administrator is employed by a company working in the education sector that either had a relationship with, or attempted to establish a relationship with the administrator's school district, there may result strong suggestions of mixed motives and even lead to the administrator and the company being accused of unethical behavior. Intimations of favoritism, fair or not, can best be avoided by a district policy that limits employment of a school official by a company doing business with the district for one or two years subsequent to departure from the district.

A perhaps obvious corollary of this policy would be one that prohibits school officials from having a financial interest in any company contracting with the district. Such a policy would have to be carefully designed to protect the rights of employees. For example, it would not be unthinkable that a school administrator might own stock in IBM. Purchase of computer equipment by the district from IBM ought not jeopardize the employment of a school administrator. A policy requiring public disclosure of such an investment might be fair to everyone.

DESIGNING THE BIDDING PROCESS

Once the decision to contract for a school district service has been made, steps must be taken to assure that the bidding process achieves a result that is congruent with the goals of the district in moving toward hiring a private provider. Effective bidding requires quality specifications, adequate advertising for bids, the development of a common understanding with bidders, careful analysis of bid proposals, and an open award process. Each state has its own particular requirements for bidding by public agencies, which local districts translate into operating procedures. School officials, perhaps with the assistance of the school district's attorney, will need to review these requirements and incorporate their provisions within the process of bidding as it unfolds. There are, however, some generic requirements of good bidding that can be outlined here.

Specifications

Obviously a school district has little chance of getting what it desires unless it defines its needs properly. This is done through the process of developing the specifications for the work to be done. The specifications contained in the invitation to bid (ITB) or request for proposals (RFP) enable vendors to determine whether they are interested in performing the service and whether they have or can acquire the resources to make a viable proposal.

As a minimum the following specific information should be included in the request for proposal (RFP):

- the terms of the contract and the renewal provisions
- the location(s) where the service will be performed
- statistical data related to the service, such as building specifications, student participation, etc.
- a detailed description of the specific services requested
- standards of quality by which the service will be measured
- terms and conditions of responses to emergencies
- required permits and licenses
- quality assurances required of the vendor (Beales, 1994, p. 14)

It is important not to use a vendor's suggested bid specifications. If the district, after studying its own operations carefully, still feels uncomfortable about the quality or reliability of its specifications, a consultant should be employed to review and possibly expand the district's first effort.

Figure 7.3 summarizes the characteristics of effectively written specifications.

Clear: The district's expectations are written in language that is unambiguous as to its meaning.

Specific: The frequency and/or level of intensity of a service and the standards by which quality will be measured are unequivocal and subject to independent verification by a neutral third party such as an arbitrator or judge who might be asked to resolve a conflict.

Accurate: Data regarding the scope of services requested are carefully validated. Careful attention must be paid to the accuracy of the specifications since changes made after a contract has been awarded can increase costs significantly.

Realistic: Sometimes it is necessary to strike a balance between preferences and practicality. It may be the district's desire to achieve a very high standard of service, a standard far higher than it has been achieving. That is admirable. However, if the standards set cannot be met by several vendors, the district faces a choice between having only one bidder (the "private monopoly" described above) or going back to providing the service itself, probably at a standard lower than a realistic standard for bidders might have provided.

Anticipatory: Inevitably, problems will arise. Some can be anticipated; some cannot. It is necessary to define the vendor's full responsibility for prompt resolution of problems, known and unknown, and to identify financial responsibility for the resolution of problems. Specific procedures for the resolution of disputes between the vendor and the district must be specified.

Figure 7.3. *Testing for Effective Specifications.*

Bidding

It is in the district's interest to get as large a pool of competent bidders as possible. It is wise to seek out possible bidders through telephone calls and encourage them to submit a proposal and to advertise the bid request in publications that have a special focus (e.g., journals relating to food service, bus transportation, etc.). This approach is far more likely to assist the district in achieving its goals than advertising in the local papers and waiting to see what happens.

It is also helpful to host a bidder's conference prior to publishing the ITB or an RFP. At this meeting potential vendors can ask questions and, more importantly, make suggestions regarding how the bid proposal might be defined. An open meeting of this kind is far more acceptable than the possibly collusive practice of sitting down with one likely bidder and using this company's ideas in establishing the bid specifications. This meeting will give the district a realistic picture of how many bidders may be able and willing to submit proposals based on various scenarios for the final bid specifications. This might be viewed as an absolute necessity if the district is going into contracting a particular service for the first time (Savas, 1987, p. 269).

One important issue for discussion at such a meeting might be the duration of the contract. From the school district's point of view it might be desirable to have a relatively short contract since the opportunity to rebid a contract puts pressure on the vendor to keep costs low and quality high.

However, vendors may need to make a significant capital investment to take over a government operation. Too short a contract would make it economically impossible to make the significant investment necessary to bid on the contract. It is also important to remember that a short contract can work to the vendor's benefit. If a profit isn't made quickly, the vendor can refuse to offer a contract renewal. A quick disappearance by the company after a contentious community debate about privatizing can be embarrassing to the district. Therefore, a conversation with potential bidders might help achieve the proper balance district and vendor need in designing the duration of a contract.

Bonding requirements are another issue that need careful analysis by the district before a requirement is promulgated. A *bid bond* affirms the intention of the contractor to carry out the terms and conditions of the bid or proposal if it is awarded or risk losing the face value of the bond.

A *performance bond* insures that, should the contractor be unable to carry out the contract for its full term, the insurance company issuing the bond will step in and make sure the contract is fulfilled by some other contractor at no additional cost to the district. Obviously both types of bond provide valuable assurances to the district. Small companies, however, especially those that are relatively new and without a significant track record, may not be able to secure a performance bond, or the high cost of such a bond for the small company may realistically inhibit its ability to make a bid or proposal. The district will need to balance assurances it would like to have with the likely effects of a high cost performance bond on potential bidders. The district may itself choose to pay for the bond in order to assure a larger number of bids, especially from newer firms.

Selecting a Contractor

Each state has its own laws regarding bidding processes and the awarding of bids. Obviously local laws must control. Bids for service contracts often have different requirements than bids for construction projects, or the purchase of products since the law usually recognizes that more is involved in a service relationship than lowest price. (In fact, one of W. Edwards Deming's fourteen principles of Total Quality Management recommends that businesses ignore lowest price in making purchase decisions. Public school districts have considerably less flexibility in this regard than private businesses.)

If price is not the only legal criterion that will govern selection of a contractor, it is important for district officials to identify the factors they will consider in making a selection. It would be foolhardy to choose the lowest proposal absent reliable information about the capacity of a potential vendor to provide quality service at the price bid.

It would also be important to know whether the bidder can supply evidence of successfully providing a similar service for another governmental agency, preferably a school district. Therefore, references will be an important piece of information to review. District officials will also want to look at the work plan of the potential vendor. This task becomes more daunting when dealing with companies that manage the full instructional program (EMOs) since most of these firms are so new that they lack a history of continuous success elsewhere.

Table 7.2.

Criterion	Weight	Score*	Weighted Score
Bid price	.45	3	1.35
Qualifications	.20	2	.40
Performance standards	.20	1	.20
Use of former district employees	.15	0	.00
Total	100%		1.95

*Note: 1 = low, 3 = high.

Therefore, at the bidder's conference it would be advisable to show to all potential bidders the criteria that will be considered and the weight that will be given to each of the designated criteria. Table 7.2 illustrates a method that might be designed to evaluate bid proposals.

Obviously, the criteria against which the district wishes to evaluate proposals must be determined by the value system of the district. For example, a district might want to evaluate the extent to which a bidder has employed minorities and females as workers and supervisors. It might want to give some points for experience in working specifically in a school district. The basic requirement is that the criteria must meet legal tests of reasonableness and appropriateness.

It is not likely that a contract to provide educational services, either for a single subject such as a foreign language or the instructional program of a school or district, can be subject to price-only competitive bidding. The goals and strategies of major corporations such as Edison and EAI are so different that an individual judgment must be made as to the needs of the district and the capacities and strategies of each company. However, this conclusion does not obviate the need to do all the preliminary planning that would define exactly what the district is looking for and how it will make a determination as to whether a private company has the solutions needed.

DESIGNING THE TERMS AND CONDITIONS OF THE CONTRACT

Savas (1987, p. 269) describes three types of agreements that might be developed when contracting for a service:

(1) *Fixed fee plus costs:* This approach lacks incentives for the company to achieve efficiencies. It is guaranteed a fee, and all of its out-of-pocket costs are guaranteed as well.

(2) *Fixed fee with incentives for system performance:* This approach allows the company the opportunity to achieve a bonus based on a known performance standard. For example, many road building contracts call for a set fee to build the road but offer a bonus if the road is completed earlier than the target date. The earlier the road is finished, the more money a company can make. In a school setting a company might be paid a bonus if no buses are cited by the state police during an inspection period.

(3) *Pure incentive:* This is the format preferred by some EMOs. As a condition of employment they will ask that all the district's revenues be turned over to the company. They offer to manage and improve district operations with these funds and still achieve an excess of revenues over expenditures, which shall constitute their profit. This approach has caused EAI problems in both Baltimore and Hartford because the terms of their contract called for periodic payments to reimburse the company for computers and other instructional equipment purchased by the company to deliver their program, payments that both districts said they were unable or unwilling to make.

The fixed fee plus incentive approach seems the most advantageous. It gives the district reliable figures toward which it can budget and avoids the natural suspicion that arises among even supportive board members and community residents regarding what secret legerdemain the company is employing to maximize their profits. A drawback is the possible incentive for the company to sacrifice quality in areas that are difficult to measure or that have not been included as standards of performance in the work specifications.

Attention must also be paid in the contract to issues related to insurance and liability. The contract should require that the contractor maintain proper insurance coverages as defined. It should also have the burden of maintaining control of its own employees. The whole purpose of these requirements is to avoid liability shifting from the contractor to the public body with the deep pockets. Indemnification may also be negotiated against third party claims by employees of the contractor or its subcontractors.

MONITORING THE CONTRACT

School district officials have the ultimate accountability for the effectiveness of all school district programs and services and are being called on by the public to take these accountability responsibilities more and more seriously. The need to monitor a contract with a vendor is part of a total and ongoing evaluation responsibility.

This responsibility can be most effectively carried out if the initial work of defining outcomes and standards of performance has been scrupulously carried out. Both parties then know what is expected of the contractor.

Rehfuss (1989, p. 8) describes three elements of a comprehensive monitoring system:

- contractor reports
- inspections
- citizen input

Each of these functions should be defined in the contract: the frequency and type of contractor information that will be required; the type of site visits district personnel are authorized to make; and the office, school district, or contractor to which formal complaints can be registered and at which they will be compiled. All of these elements should be measured against performance standards identified in the contract.

There are two goals for careful monitoring of contracts: assurance that defined services are being provided at the standard of quality called for in the contract and assurance that the district is getting what it is paying for; that is, that wage rates being charged to the district are actually being paid to contractor employees and that all materials and services are provided at the standard of quality called for in the contract (Rehfuss, 1989, p. 11).

TERMINATING THE CONTRACT

As has been pointed out before, it is ordinarily in the best interest of the district to write a contract for a short term. The pressure on the company to do a good job appears to be higher when it must face the prospect of renewal in the near future. However, the desirability of a short-term contract needs to be balanced by the recognition that a company will not agree to a short-term contract if it must make a significant capital investment to take on a contract with a school district. The bidder's conference can be used to determine the length of contract that represents a fair balance between the desires of the district and the needs of the company.

An even more important consideration is the benefit to the district of the freedom to terminate a contract *without cause* with a reasonable notice period of 30–90 days (Beales & O'Leary, p. 9). Given the abrupt terminations that EAI has experienced in Baltimore and Hartford, it may prove increasingly difficult in the future to get companies to agree to such a bailout provision. However, if a company is doing a genuinely poor job, government officials will need the opportunity to come up with an alternate delivery system or face recall. Perhaps mutually acceptable language that would, upon official notification by the district of an intention to cancel the contract, give the company a fixed period of time to "cure" the dissatisfaction would be fair to both parties.

CONTRACTING AND COLLECTIVE BARGAINING

Approximately thirty-nine states have some form of collective bargaining for public employees. The rights of public employees under these laws differ significantly from state to state. In addition these laws are always in a state of flux caused by court decisions, arbitration awards, new legislation, and so forth. For example, until very recently privatization of a service was a mandatory subject of bargaining in Michigan. It is not any longer. It was recently removed as an area subject to negotiations.

It is not possible to advise districts specifically about how to deal with collective bargaining issues. However, it is possible to call attention to the absolute importance of understanding state laws regarding collective bargaining before embarking on a privatization initiative. Mistakes in this area can be expensive to repair and contribute to the community turmoil surrounding a switch to a private company. There are examples of school districts that have entered into a privatization agreement only to face a strike by employees before the contract with the private vendor started. The strike then led to a court injunction that required the district to pay the company with which it had contracted for service and also pay former employees until the courts determined whether the district had acted legally in signing a contract with a private vendor.

A district will need to make an *a priori* decision regarding which requirements it will seek to impose on a contracting company regarding the hiring and payment of its former employees. It might choose any one of the three following positions:

- Require the vendor to give first right of refusal to current employees and also require that current salaries and benefits be maintained ("red lined") at the time of hire. Labor cost savings for the vendor would then have to come through attrition of current employees.
- Require that current employees have the right of first refusal for jobs with the new company but make no requirements regarding the level of salary and benefits.
- Make no requirements regarding current employees.

By the value system of most people the first option is the most humane. However it may raise financial and legal issues that will inhibit bidding on the contract. "If the contractor intends to, or is required to, offer the public employees first right to employment under the contract, under a new National Labor Relations Board (NLRB) decision [Canteen Company, 317 NLRB No 153, June 30, 1995], the contractor may have a duty to bargain the *initial terms* of employment with the union representing those employees" (presentation to Pinckney School Board). Such an obligation may have some impact on the number of companies willing to bid on the contract. Companies that understand these recent decisions will be scrupulous in making clear what they view as their obligations to employees before a contract is finalized.

SUMMARY

Since contracts are legal documents, it is wise for a district contemplating privatizing a function to acquire competent legal advice in generating a contract. Yet many of the judgments that lead to a contract are essentially policy and business decisions, not legal choices. Knowledgeable board members and administrators will study carefully issues related to defining bid specifications, determining bonding requirements, establishing performance criteria, and understanding collective bargaining obligations so as to achieve a quality service at a reasonable cost. Maximizing the number of companies that can bid or make a proposal on a project may be the best route to achieving this balance of cost and quality.

CHAPTER 8

Privatization in the 21st Century

"We provide privately run magnet schools for public systems. If Edison can prove money can be made by creating quality public schools, more private companies will join the handful that are in the education business. We have started down the pioneering and somewhat bloody road. This is not just playful futurism."

Chris Whittle, Founder, The Edison Project, *Detroit Free Press,* June 6, 1996

SOCIAL CHANGE: THE ANTECEDENTS OF PRIVATIZATION

It is premature to anticipate the death of public education. It is, of course, perfectly reasonable to anticipate fundamental changes in public education, both in the content of instruction and, perhaps more pervasively, in the delivery system. Many of these changes have already begun, some not so recently.

Not-for-profit private schools, many run by religious groups, have been in existence for most of the twentieth century. Voucher programs were tried in the 1960s in Alum Rock, California. Performance contracting with private companies for instructional improvement was popular in the 1970s. Companies provided curriculum design, staff training, and, occasionally, direct instruction of students. Private for-profit schools, now about 3–5% of all schools, have been in existence for decades, some having been established as early as the 1940s (Miller, 1995). Perhaps only charter schools, entities financed by public funds and operated by citizens, not government bodies, have no longstanding historical precedent. Nevertheless, the spirit of the nineties and the coming millennium calls for significant, perhaps fundamental, change. Trends that in other decades were experiments of interest to only a few have now become mainstream ideas in the public's search for quality education at reasonable cost. These trends toward innovation are driven by at least three important forces: technology, popular ideology, and economics.

TECHNOLOGY AND EDUCATIONAL CHANGE

The impact of technology on school organization and structures has only begun to be felt. The Internet, which makes information available to everyone, everywhere, will further deepen the gap between education and schooling. As portable and laptop computers become an increasingly common tool for students—they are now required for *all* students at a few colleges and universities—the role of teachers, the function of traditional classrooms, and the design of the curriculum will undergo significant change. In a world in which 40% of American households have computers and more and more businesses are discovering the Internet as an instrument of commerce, students (and parents) will increasingly be aware of the options for learning outside the classroom. For example, in May 1996 the Bell & Howell corporation held its annual meeting for shareholders on the Internet. Participants could hear the meeting free of charge after downloading from the World Wide Web site ("Firm takes it annual meeting to the Net," *Detroit Free Press*, May 16, 1996, Business Section). This virtual meeting suggests the road that will soon be traveled in decoupling events from places. "School" will be everywhere. Only the need for education to play a custodial role for children while parents are at work, no insignificant responsibility, and the difficulty that many school districts face in acquiring money for technology are slowing down what would otherwise be even more fundamental modification in the delivery system of public education.

IDEOLOGY AND EDUCATIONAL CHANGE

Many forces are also converging to shape the attitudes of education consumers, most particularly parents, about what they want from public education. Choices are everywhere for the American consumer, brought on to some extent by the development of a global economy. If the potential purchaser is unhappy with the price, quality, or design of Chrysler, Ford, or General Motors cars, there are unlimited options among the vehicles produced in Japan, Sweden, Great Britain, Germany, Korea, and elsewhere. These options are available down the street.

Selective marketing drives product development. Large producers of goods try to customize their products so that there is something available for the particular tastes of the young, the middle aged, and the old; the poor, the middle class, and the wealthy; Blacks, Whites, Asians, Hispanics, and other ethnic groups. The fastest growing sector of the economy is small business. Here entrepreneurs exploit "niche markets," responding to the special needs of customers, whether business enterprises or consumers.

The predominant metaphor of social integration has changed. Government no longer seeks programs and policies that will foster the "melting pot" concept of American society. Perhaps the "salad bowl" image, separate segments of society joined together in a common interest, is more appropriate, but that concept also has many weaknesses. Significant proportions of the population wish to protect their national language and customs, their religious identity and traditions, and/or their moral value systems. When deeply held convictions on the part of these different segments of the adult population conflict, public schools are often thrown into community controversies. Many of these disputes arise over differences in opinion about the role of schools in exposing students to ideas, values, beliefs, and traditions different from those taught at home. However, large segments of the community continue to believe that the role of the school is simply to inculcate the majority culture.

The explosion of interest in charter schools—forty states had or were considering the implementation of such entities in 1996—is a reflection of the general trend toward "personalized" education, a school for every interest and taste. The rapid growth in home schooling also indicates that more and more parents want to have a larger voice in shaping the type of education provided to their children. The doubling of the membership of the American Association of Educators in Private Practice further illustrates the diversity of the education marketplace that is developing.

Most people living in or close to a large city are periodically exposed to news stories about parents standing on long lines for days or even weeks, despite cold weather, snow storms, or other inconveniences, to get a place for their children in magnet and other special schools. The students who are accepted have happy parents. The parents of those who are rejected, despite their personal demonstration of a willingness to suffer great personal discomfort to achieve quality education for their children, are angry. For them, public education appears to be a heartless bureaucracy. Reading about such events in the daily newspaper, the average citizen, with a modern customer mentality, is nonplused: if the school is so desirable in its present incarnation, why doesn't the district create more of them?

Successful leaders of public education in the 21st century will turn away from the illogic of making parents compete for spaces in schools that are viewed as successful. They will increasingly develop techniques for more rapidly reacting to an environment that demands multiple options for learning. An enhancement to this move toward flexible solutions will include the just emerging involvement of the private sector in helping to create alternative delivery systems. Companies are beginning to do this because it is in their own economic interests to do so. The Ford Motor Company is sponsoring a charter school in Dearborn, Michigan, for students who aspire to work in the skilled trades. Ford hopes that this school will help assure a competent supply of potential employees at a time of a generational turnover in the factories because of retirements. "Company sponsored schools (will) . . . help guarantee qualified applicants (and) put more pressure on existing school districts to meet the challenge" (*Oakland Press*, May 3, 1996, Editorial).

ECONOMICS AND EDUCATIONAL CHANGE

A few years ago an executive of one of the major automobile manufacturing companies was being interviewed on the radio. He was asked about the significant increase in price that each new model car carried. He was reminded that most studies had shown a declining income for many Americans when cost of living was considered, thereby making it harder and harder for most Americans to afford a new car. How would the automobile companies be able to sell new cars in the future, he was asked.

He responded by admitting that the interviewer had raised a real problem and that the auto companies had yet to come up with a strategy that would recognize a phenomena that he called "the pooring of America." Obviously the car companies have been struggling to decrease manufacturing costs by increasing productivity, and American buyers have been coping with rising prices by going deeper into debt to purchase the vehicles that they desire or moving to leasing, which requires less money to initiate the transaction.

This apparent reduction in the real buying power of wages, especially for the middle and lower classes, has occurred at the same time that the public has grown increasingly disenchanted with government and seeks smaller government at every level. These two phenomena are probably interrelated. Citizens who see their buying power dissipating yet who are faced with constantly escalating taxes, with little perceived direct benefit to them, are inevitably going to challenge the tax rate to which they are subject. In the spring of 1996 the state of Nebraska set new caps on property taxes and capped spending increases for schools at 2% for 1997 and mandated no increases for 1998 except for adjustments for increased enrollment. The Education Committee chairwoman in the state Senate attributed the action to the reality that "80 percent of the people in Nebraska do not have kids in the public schools, and 65 percent of their property taxes go for education" (Archer, 1996, p. 11).

The federal government has been the primary, though not exclusive, target of citizen dissatisfaction with taxes and government efficiency and effectiveness. The conventional political response has been to develop proposals to devolve many responsibilities formerly held by the federal government back to the states, most especially two very large and expensive programs, welfare and Medicaid. Though most current governors seem to embrace these changes, many will not be in office when the inevitable fiscal downturn hits the country and the limited funds in block grants and state revenues leave needy citizens unserved. These changes, plus the public's apparent solution of choice for increased crime rates, building and operating more prisons, will leave state governments more strapped for funds to finance public education. School policymakers and school leaders have no choice. They *will* find new ways to provide quality services at the least cost since the funds available to them seem likely to decline under almost any school funding scenario.

PRIVATIZATION AS A STRATEGY FOR THE FUTURE

There are any number of proposals to remedy the ills of public education. For a very few opinion leaders complete elimination of public education is necessary before more promising forms of educational delivery can flourish. Perhaps widely published author Myron Lieberman speaks most frequently, if not most eloquently, for that body of opinion. Though one of his books has pronounced the death of public education and offered an autopsy (1993), a reading of the book shows it to be more a plan of war to bring about such a result than an analysis of an extinction. This view does not seem to be widely shared, at least not its militancy.

More commonly held strategies seek to create alternative ways to provide education and other public services now viewed as the primary role of government. Tuition voucher proposals, often portrayed as poison pills for public education, try to use an open market strategy to reduce government's role in education, not necessarily eliminate it as a school service provider. By itself widespread use of vouchers would not destroy public education, though the resulting effect on education could be dramatic and socially undesirable. Even Nathan Glazer, the eminent Harvard professor and long-time supporter of quality education for all children, came to the conclusion over a decade ago that public schools were incapable of accommodating the "conflicts of values in the country today between the religious and the secular, the permissive and the traditional, those seeking experiences and those seeking security and stability" and advocated for vouchers (Glazer, 1983, p. 100). More about that later.

The focus of this book has been on contracting, or "outsourcing," as a form of privatization rather than more radical forms of privatization such as tuition vouchers, since there are serious and unresolved federal constitution questions regarding vouchers, especially the use of vouchers at denominational schools. The question then is whether outsourcing, since it is argued that it is basically a tactical question, reflects the public will and belief systems and whether it is likely to increase in importance in the future. The issue can be analyzed in summary fashion from a public policy, financial, and political perspective.

PRIVATIZING AS A PUBLIC POLICY ISSUE

It can be argued that privatization as contracting is no longer a policy "issue." The expanding use of private companies to provide support services in education has been going on for a very long time. Were

America still a country that was expanding geographically to such an extent that new school districts were being created, there would probably be little public interest in whether a new district contracted for bus, cafeteria, or building maintenance services. Even unions would probably seek little role in such a debate.

Should the Edison Project and other companies be able to deliver on their promises of better education for less money, there will be less and less controversy about employing a private company to manage the instructional program in a public school or school district. Such a step will seem less and less a "radical" solution. Parents and citizens throughout the country will grow increasingly comfortable with school district/private company partnerships.

It is the transition from government provided to privatized services that raises issues of public policy. What will be the incentives for and barriers to privatization that a school board will need to consider in the next decade?

INCENTIVES TO CHANGE

The incentives to change have been discussed in Chapter 5:

- improved accountability
- enhanced cost efficiency
- sharper mission focus
- innovative thinking

These incentives for districts to use private companies will continue into the foreseeable future.

BARRIERS TO CHANGE

Reaction to Corporate Downsizing

Patrick Buchanan, though unsuccessful in his primary campaign to be nominated as presidential candidate by the Republican Party in 1996, touched a raw nerve in a large segment of the American population. He articulated the agony of layoffs, the result of the widespread "downsizing" of American industry. U.S. Labor Secretary Robert Reich, later supported by U.S. Treasury Secretary Robert Rubin, called for a change in tax policy that would favor companies that were willing to protect their employees from such dramatic events. These layoffs often occurred after employees spent many years with a company and occasionally were implemented shortly before the retirement of some employees. There appears to be a growing public dissatisfaction with such actions, a dissatisfaction that could undermine any local school district effort to terminate a service provided by district employees without the most careful consideration of their future employment, either with the district in another capacity or with the contractor.

Perceived Conflict between Profit and Good Works

There is a broad perception that public work produces a public good. The very nature of public work has long implied that workers who choose to labor in the public sector do so for somewhat altruistic reasons. For decades in the first half of the twentieth century typically low wages for public workers reinforced the notion that the satisfaction, and the security, of public service made up, at least somewhat, for the low wages such jobs typically paid. Though public sector wages caught up with, and in some cases, surpassed many comparable positions in business and industry, this halo effect of public work still exists. There will undoubtedly be some members of the community, reflecting a body of opinion throughout the nation, who will feel that hiring a profit-making company will change government's focus from public interest to profit. Visions of mindless cost cutting in the service of investor returns are not too hard to engender in many citizens, especially parents worried whether their children will get the best education possible.

What is often forgotten is that good service is the best guarantee of profits. The conviction of United Way of America's William Aramony, whose salary of over $390,000 and flights on the Concorde for pleasure as well as business, suggests that public and non-profit sector employees have no exclusive hold on the virtue of self-abnegation.

Fear for the Future of Public Education

There are many reasons why public education has been a respected institution for over a century. Many immigrants, the forebears of all citizens, owe their success in America to the opportunities for education and training received in public schools. Though significant dissatisfaction with public education is often captured in public opinion polls, the public still appears to prefer to fix rather than dismantle the nation's educational system. Any step by a school district that suggests that the final intention and result of a privatizing effort could be the destruction of public education will tap a reservoir of support that may not be easily perceived when the focus of the press is on dissatisfaction. Phi Delta Kappa's Center on National Education Policy (1996) has noted that "Americans developed public schools to unify our nation and to provide for the common good. If we proceed with proposals that are not true to the spirit of this history, then we may lose the very features of public schooling that our early leaders believed were necessary to form a strong, cohesive, and just nation" (p. 22).

Education as Community

Hundreds of school districts across the nation are named Community Schools, preceded by the name of the village, town, city, or county. They represent a universal concern for all citizens. Schools are the largest investment made in common by all citizens since everyone pays some property tax to support schools, and property tax still provides some support for public schools in most states. The Mott Foundation has spent millions of dollars encouraging the use of schools for community events and community purposes. Many school districts have responded to this call. Whether the major focus of a community is on the high school football team, SAT scores, or both, many people, satisfied or dissatisfied, usually are concerned about their schools.

Perhaps more important, more and more school districts are recognizing the truth of the African proverb that "It takes a community to educate a child." Some critics of privatization see the effort to substitute employees hired by an outside company for district-hired employees as a deliberately imposed breech in the implied social contract between a community's children and its adults.

Those who are successful in moving ahead with a contract for services will be able to demonstrate how privatization represents a better way for the community to focus its resources on its most precious asset, its children.

PRIVATIZING AS A FINANCIAL ISSUE

As has been shown, civic government moved much more rapidly than school districts into privatizing some functions and also facilities, and some studies have shown cost savings among a significant number of government entities that have privatized services. The Touche Ross (1987) "Opinion Survey of City and County Governments on Their Use of Privatization and Their Infrastructure Needs" found that "Forty percent of the governments that contracted services out for this reason (to cut costs) saved at least 20 percent and 10 percent saved 40 percent or more" (p. 2). Similar notable cost savings were achieved from facilities that were privatized.

Compiled financial data regarding the effects of contracting as a cost reduction measure in school districts are difficult to find. The Mackinac Center for Public Policy, in association with the Reason Foundation in California, has published a series of monographs, many authored or co-authored by Janet Beales, regarding the effects of contracting in public education. Several of these publications have been referenced in the text. They represent some of the earliest and most complete work regarding privatization in public education. However, they are heavily anecdotal in discussing cost saving possibilities. Compiled data about cost savings that are presented tend to be at the industry level and drawn from materials written by others. Successful cases of privatizing in school districts abound in the publications, but negative experiences are nowhere to be found. Since the sponsors of the work support increased privatization in public education, such characteristics are not surprising.

Yet there are apparently negative experiences, since a study of privatization among school districts conducted by the National School Boards Association (NSBA) found that "While cost savings is the primary reason given by 45 percent of the survey respondents for privatizing school services, only one-third of that group indicate some savings has actually been realized" (NSBA, 1995b, p. 11). An attempt to analyze this data further was thwarted because the survey results were not kept by NSBA. The best statewide study of privatization in the public sector, done in Texas, contains comprehensive information about the prevalence of contracting in seven traditional school services, such as food service, transportation, health, and medical services but provides virtually no financial data about cost savings that were realized (Taebel and Brenner, 1994).

The logic of financial savings through contracting seems unassailable. If the district can define the full range of services it wants and then seeks bids or quotations, it can make its own decision about the wisdom of contracting and the tradeoffs between dollar savings and the costs in community peace and employee morale. Seeking bids or proposals from private companies allows the district to establish a baseline cost to provide a service. It fosters rethinking of how personnel and technology are deployed to accomplish predetermined goals. Though he later found himself in conflict with EAI over contract payment issues, Mayor Kurt Schmoke of Baltimore was originally a big booster of privatization because he found that schools working with EAI "looked more inviting. . . . There are more computers, the buildings are cleaner, the food service is better, and all the support services are running more efficiently" (Goldberg, 1995, p. 237). It is quite likely that the service level established by EAI will significantly affect the level to be expected in the future from district employees. More significantly, as the standards rise in an increasingly larger number of districts, they begin to become the new norms for all districts.

Studies regarding cost savings attributable to privatizing must be done at the state and national level so as to provide a better database for decision making. State superintendent and school board associations, perhaps working in tandem, would seem logical parties to initiate such studies. In addition to collecting data about the cost saving effects of an initial contract with a vendor, much more needs to be learned about the longer term effects of a privatization decision. For example, do most contractors offer a second contract similar to the first, with normal increases proposed for cost-of-living and unanticipated situations, or do they significantly increase the proposal the second time around, especially if they are in a "monopsonistic" (Bailey, 1991, p. 237) situation; that is, the only viable private provider in the area? It will also be important to learn what happens to district employees who are hired by the contractor under the provisions of the first contract. Do most employees who want to stay with the private provider have the opportunity to do so? What happens to their compensation in the company's second contract with the district? Ultimately data needs to be generated that are objective and comprehensive.

In light of the pervasiveness of contracting in American public education today, it is foolish to ask whether privatization is good or bad. What is needed and is beginning to emerge is information that describes under what circumstances and conditions privatization can be a prudent step for a school district, but far more data are needed.

The best decisions will be made by districts that look at this issue dispassionately long before any financial crisis moves them precipitously to find a "port in a storm" of red ink. The history of privatization by the federal government is rife with stories of contractor abuse and will be used by some to attempt to discredit contracting. Such situations tell more about government oversight of contractors, or the lack thereof, than they do about privatization. A recent excoriation of New York City Mayor Rudolph Giuliani's attempts to privatize a home relief program for single adults by editors of the *New York Times*, an effort that engendered problems of political favoritism if not corruption, reinforced "the perils of privatizing traditional government services" (Editorial, March 30, 1996).

But bad practices do not make imperfect policy. Market solutions are neither inherently good nor evil. As the late economist Arthur Okun noted, "The market needs a place and the market needs to be kept in its place" (in Kuttner, p. 313). School districts that study carefully the use of public-private partnerships will avoid the excesses of rhetoric from either side of the debate about privatization.

PRIVATIZING AS A POLITICAL ISSUE

A whole chapter in this book has been devoted to dealing with political concerns raised by contracting for services at the local level. There are clearly larger political issues affecting the broader movement to privatize public education that should be noted, though they are not the primary focus of this book.

There is a body of opinion that sees the privatizing movement as part of a grand scheme to dismantle the liberal democratic state (Murphy, 1996). This is a United States version of what has happened in Great Britain in the last decade or so and a reflection of the breakup of bureaucratic government around the world, especially in the Soviet Union and the members of its Eastern Bloc of countries. The Republican Party in the United States has been particularly dedicated to market approaches to improving education by promoting such alternatives as charter schools, vouchers, and tuition tax credits. The nature of privatization in the 21st century will be driven largely by decisions made by courts and legislatures at the state and national level.

If the political methodology of choice for reforming the system is to "deregulate" it by offering opportunities for parents to send their children to schools operated outside the government-run educational system as it is now composed, then privatization in all its forms will probably flourish. Though many people retain a deep appreciation for the contributions of the public education system as it has functioned in the past, their present inclinations, formed from living in a culture of choice, are likely to be to seek out a "boutique" form of education that meets the specific needs of their children as they view them. Therefore, many are likely to support proposals that redefine how children may access education at public expense. By creating alternative schools, magnet schools, schools within schools, schools located in rented spaces in office buildings near where parents work, and other real options to the "one size fits all" model of public education that has endured for so long, schools will be able to respond to the tastes of the emerging generation of parents. Contracting with a private company to operate one or more schools within a district seems a sensible option to create choice for parents and children and to expand options for improving instruction.

Susan Wadsworth, director of the non-partisan polling group Public Agenda, has described support for public schools as "very fragile" as a result of a poll of adults in the United States. Only 48% of respondents supported fixing public schools, either by overhauling them or giving them more money (*New York Times,* April 9, 1995). Publications that defend the achievements of public education mentioned in previous chapters and the annual reports of Gerald Bracey in the *Phi Delta Kappan* magazine seem to have had little effect on the widespread feeling that schools are failing to carry out their mission to prepare children for the future.

A court challenge to Milwaukee's legislation that permitted vouchers to be used at private schools seems likely to work its way to the U.S. Supreme Court. The Pennsylvania Court has already ruled about the permissibility of involuntarily moving teachers out of the building to be run by a private company and replacing them by teachers selected by the company. Challenges to a California law that prohibits supervisory positions from being occupied by non-district employed personnel seem likely.

Lost in all the public/private political and legal debates are other substantive issues. Many minorities, especially Afro-Americans, who had their employment opportunities limited by generations of discrimination, first began to break into middle class life through public employment since public entities were more easily challenged on fair employment practices than private ones. The "market" approach to solving public education's assumed cost and productivity problems raises other issues of public policy that cannot be ignored but should not be thought of in simplistic terms either. The employment gains of Blacks and other minorities must be continued. Federal and state law, as well as enlightened corporate policy, can be marshaled to manage this issue in a constructive way.

The first response to desegregation in the south was the creation of private academies, private schools run at private expense. The charter school and tuition voucher movements raise many issues related to equity and to the type of society they are likely to foster. In the 1960s the Kerner Commission warned that we are "moving toward two societies, one white, one black" (National Advisory Commission on Civil Disorders, 1968). State laws invariably require that charter schools be open to all who apply, even mandating lottery selection when the number of students exceeds the school's capacity. But school location and issues related to transportation, often not provided at public expense, operate to create an invisible barrier to many children, especially those in the inner city. On the other hand, studies in Michigan have shown that 40% of all charter schools are located in the inner city itself, a reflection of substantive dissatisfaction among parents about the quality, and often safety, of public schools, especially those located in the inner city.

Courts will be required to examine carefully the equities involved in further expansion of the market as a vehicle for improving public schools. Meanwhile, contracting for educational and support services will grow, and current barriers to public/private partnerships that are embedded in legislation are likely to be modified if not eliminated in response to public demands for more choices.

SCHOOL DISTRICT PRIVATIZATION IN THE FUTURE

It is sometimes difficult to distinguish a fad from a movement. Ideas can capture the imagination of many people for a short period of time and then disappear from the landscape almost completely. As divorce rates escalated in the 1970s and 1980s some were questioning the viability of permanent marriage as an institution, especially as much larger percentages of the people were living into old age. Today practically every politician is singing the virtues of "family values." Communal living seemed to represent a new wave of the future as the 1960s came to an end. Many of the young people involved in these experiments now live in the suburbs and sell stocks and bonds.

This book has attempted to demonstrate that privatization is closer to a movement than a fad since it represents the logical extension of many social, economic, and philosophical trends that have been going on for several decades. However, it is still unclear how far these trends will evolve in changing American institutions. Republicans seized control of the U.S. House and Senate in the 1994 elections and the governor's office and legislatures of many states. Therefore, there has been fertile soil for discussions of market solutions. Future elections may tell more whether privatization is a societal direction or a briefly popular aberration.

However, virtually no one predicts that the amount of contracting or outsourcing already present in education and other governmental services is likely to recede measurably. The somewhat bipolar demands of the American public for services, or at least payments, from the federal government yet the companion desire to shrink the size of the federal budget, reduce the deficit, and lower taxes have led to an ever increasing use of outsourcing by the national government. "The Government's costs for outside, or contract, employees keeps rising. . . . The dollar value of Federal service contracts with private companies has risen more than 3.5% a year since 1993, to $114 billion last year" (*New York Times*, March 18, 1996). It seems inevitable that this trend will continue into the 21st century.

RECOMMENDATIONS FOR DISTRICTS ENTERING PRIVATIZATION

Privatization, especially contracting, will be successful in school districts in the years ahead if school districts use the same careful thought processes that they recommend to their students when solving academic problems. Some of the major areas for consideration are the following:

(1) Clarify why the district is choosing a privatized solution. Districts need to have a positive notion of what privatization can accomplish. The Hartford, Connecticut School District had a major economic

problem and was thrashing about for any life jacket that would secure the financial condition of the district. The *New York Times* reported that "the school board, lacking the will to make tough budget decisions itself, saw Education Alternatives as a corporate angel" (March 11, 1996). Board members failed to study the issue carefully enough to know how the district was going to be "saved" and that the company was going to make a profit at the same time.

(2) Choose privatization for a positive reason, not a negative one. A few of the early adopter districts of contracting, especially contracting for instruction on a large scale, appear to have done so more for retribution against a teachers' union rather than for a rational expectation that improvement will follow. The Wilkinsburg, Pennsylvania School District chose to contract for the operation of an elementary school immediately after a contentious round of collective bargaining.

They chose a firm that had no experience in carrying out such a task. EAI and the Edison Project have well-structured instructional improvement designs. The Marriott Corporation successfully runs food service programs in all types of businesses and institutions. National Bus Company can provide references all over the country. A district should choose a vendor because there are sound reasons to believe that they can improve operations or at least maintain satisfactory services for significantly less cost.

(3) Collect as much comparable data as possible before making a decision. School districts need to disaggregate their own cost data so as to have solid information about their real in-house costs and do comparative studies among districts of similar characteristics, such as size, geographic location, labor market characteristics, etc. If another district claims cost savings through contracting, it is important to validate the similarity of circumstances so that the conclusion that the district will achieve similar gains can be confirmed. Harry Hatry has noted that "our work at the Urban Institute indicates that the appropriateness or success of using a particular privatization option is highly situational" (1991, p. 262). It is also important that data collection projects be started to document the real costs and benefits of contracting among districts with different characteristics.

(4) Try to preserve both the moral center and the financial security of the district. School districts take seriously their responsibilities to

develop both the ability of students to think and to care about their society and their fellow human beings. So too must districts maintain a moral commitment to their employees. An existing service or function probably should not be privatized if it is working well and cost savings attributable to contracting are not significant. If logic suggests that privatizing is an appropriate step, then employees deserve district support in a transition process that will be painful for them. Every effort should be made to retrain employees who would prefer to remain with the district. The most enlightened of districts will start this process long before the option of privatizing becomes a reality.

SUMMARY

The United States is now a mature nation with a stable economy.

Service quality
Standards of service will be benchmarked and costs will stabilize or decline as increasingly more districts discover that contracting can be a positive option to improve programs and services.

Private providers
The number of companies seeking to provide one or more services to school districts will continue to grow. The number of educators working as individual contractors will also grow, fostered by the growing practice of school districts to "buy out" higher priced staff. A significant number of these teachers will still want to use their talents to educate children. Districts will want to use targeted employment of private practice educators to acquire the talents of outstanding teachers without fringe benefit costs.

Parent power
As more companies enter the public education market, as school choice programs continue to expand, and as districts increasingly create more options for students, the power of parents to choose programs they, not a school district, deem appropriate for their children will increase.

State legislatures will continue the trend of fostering a market in public education. More states will pass charter school legislation. More options for students to attend public schools outside the area of residency will be defined in law.

Courts
Courts will make final decisions about how far, if at all, states may go in allowing public funds to be used at private schools.

Data
Careful research will provide data to help district officials determine which privatization efforts are likely to succeed in their environment.

Figure 8.1.   *Into the 21st Century—The Future of Privatization.*

Spectacular economic growth which will contribute to significant increases in government revenues cannot be expected. As the nation's population grows there is less to go around. All of these facts contribute to a public school system that is criticized and underfunded when compared to the investment of the gross national product of other industrialized nations.

School officials are, in general, trying their best to provide quality education for all children amidst a cacophony of values, needs, and preferences. Contracting to achieve economies and quality improvements is as logical as it is inevitable. By itself and done thoughtfully it is no threat to the tradition of American public education. It deserves support, understanding, and a fair chance when done in a humane manner.

Figure 8.1 portrays the likely future of privatizing as society enters a new millennium.

Choosing a Make or Buy Solution:
A Practitioner's Checklist

	Yes	No
The Public Solution		
Has the district sought employee advice about ways to reduce costs?	_____	_____
Has the district sought employee advice about ways to improve quality?	_____	_____
Can the district list distinct steps it has taken to improve quality or reduce costs?	_____	_____
Has the district employed a consultant to provide advice about how to save money or improve quality?	_____	_____
Has the district explored the possibility of reducing costs or improving quality by partnering with one or more other public organizations:		
one or more other school districts?	_____	_____
the city, township, or other local government structure?	_____	_____
a non-profit agency?	_____	_____
a joint powers agreement among school districts and possibly other entities?	_____	_____

	Yes	*No*
Is a preference for continuing to maintain the service as a district responsibility based on validated cost data?	_____	_____
Has a person knowledgeable in the industry been employed to confirm the accuracy of the district's cost analysis?	_____	_____

The Private Solution

Has the district assured itself that there are multiple viable bidders capable of bidding on a contract?	_____	_____
Will current school employees be encouraged to make a bid or a proposal?	_____	_____
Has the district considered seeking bids or proposals on only part of the service area so as to pilot a full implementation and create constructive competition?	_____	_____

Determining the True Cost of a Service

Have all costs directly attributable to a function in the budget been totaled (e.g., salaries)?	_____	_____
Have all costs directly assignable to a function but included in larger budget categories been disaggregated (e.g., fringe benefit costs)?	_____	_____
Have all non-personnel costs assignable to the function been included in the cost study (e.g., utilities, inventory, supplies)?	_____	_____
Have all non-salary personnel costs been recognized (overtime, unfilled positions)?	_____	_____
Has a proportion of the cost of all district offices that provide services to the function been included in the cost analysis (e.g., payroll)?	_____	_____

	Yes	*No*
Have the "opportunity costs" of using facilities and equipment for other purposes been included in the cost calculation?	_____	_____
Have the one time costs of transitioning to a private vendor been calculated:		
legal costs (including employee challenges to the contract)?	_____	_____
payment of accumulated benefits to employees?	_____	_____
unemployment benefits?	_____	_____
Has the district calculated the cost of monitoring the contract:		
the quality of services provided?	_____	_____
the terms of the contract?	_____	_____

Making a Decision to Privatize

	Yes	*No*
Does the district have a policy defining the amount of cost saving that will justify a move to outsourcing?	_____	_____
Does the district have an operational definition of the quality improvements necessary to justify privatization?	_____	_____
Does the district have any master contract provisions that would prohibit contract discussions with private vendors?	_____	_____
Has the district checked with its attorney regarding its legal authority to contract for services?	_____	_____
Has the district calculated the cost of taking back a service for which it has contracted?	_____	_____

Negotiating a Contract: A Practitioner's Checklist

Although the authors have divided this checklist into sections, assigning each item to one category, some items could be placed in more than one category.

	Yes	*No*

General

Will a contract with the company result in an overall improvement in the district's primary mission?

Will a future termination of the contract with the company result in any serious difficulties for the district?

Are there any conflicts of interest between the company or any subcontractors and any members of the school board or district administration?

Will the district maintain veto control over company efforts to cut costs?

Has a budget been established to cover the costs of conducting the due diligence process?

Is there a provision for a longitudinal study of the success of the contractor?

Will the longitudinal study be executed by an outside group and financed by the company?

	Yes	No
Are there plans for continuation of service should the company's employees engage in a work stoppage?	_____	_____

Administrative

	Yes	No
Has the chain of command between the district and the company been identified for implementing the contract?	_____	_____
Will the district be free to accept contributions and/or additional sources of revenue without sharing them with the company?	_____	_____
Will the company's implementation of contract terms be monitored? How?	_____	_____
Will the district have access to all statistical records about the company's work in the district?	_____	_____
Are the content, methods, and timing of company progress reports to the district identified?	_____	_____
Is the responsibility for complying with future legislation spelled out in the contract?	_____	_____
Have the company's responsibilities for special programs and services been identified (e.g., busing to athletic events in a transportation contract)?	_____	_____
Have the standards of performance been identified?	_____	_____
Does the contract identify the method for coordinating the company's service with other district systems and services?	_____	_____

Finance

	Yes	No
Are the amount, method, and timing of compensation for the company's effort clearly identified?	_____	_____

	Yes	*No*
Does the contract impact the district's ability to borrow?	_____	_____
Does the board retain budgeting responsibility?	_____	_____
Is the company obligated to disclose how funds were expended and what profits were made?	_____	_____
Has a method for allocating unanticipated cost savings and/or cost overruns been identified?	_____	_____
Has a list of charges for extra services been spelled out?	_____	_____
Have the ownership, maintenance, disposal, and replacement of existing district equipment been addressed?	_____	_____
Will capital investments made by the company be specifically identified and enumerated by year of installation, cost, and useful life?	_____	_____
Has the responsibility for the selection and purchase of new materials and equipment been identified?	_____	_____
Has the responsibility for paying for upgrading equipment, facilities, and/or material been identified?	_____	_____
Has a scheduled equipment replacement cycle been identified?	_____	_____
Has a method been identified for the district to acquire company purchased equipment in the event a contract is terminated?	_____	_____
Can the company sell district assets; if so, who owns the proceeds?	_____	_____
Will the types and levels of existing insurances be maintained by the company?	_____	_____
Will additional costs incurred by the district as a result of the contract be paid for by the company?	_____	_____

	Yes	*No*
Can the district's agents conduct an audit of the company's operations, as well as affiliates, for compliance with the contract and the district's legal obligations?	_____	_____
If the cost of the district's audit increases, will the company pay a proportionate share of increased audit costs?	_____	_____
Does the contract identify the method for coordinating the company's service with other district systems and services?	_____	_____

Personnel

	Yes	*No*
Has the employer of record (district or contractor) been identified?	_____	_____
What involvement does the district have in the selection and placement of the manager or workers?	_____	_____
Have supervisory responsibilities for district and company employees been articulated in the contract?	_____	_____
Will the district have access to the company's evaluation of its district assigned staff?	_____	_____
Is the company mandated to perform criminal checks of all district assigned staff?	_____	_____
Is the company mandated to perform health checks of all district assigned staff?	_____	_____
Is the "Management Rights" clause in the employees' collective bargaining agreement broad enough to allow the district to outsource a service without prior negotiations with the union?	_____	_____
Is there specific language in the union contract that either allows or prohibits the performance of bargaining unit work by non-unit employees or contractors?	_____	_____

	Yes	*No*
Has the district prepared a strategy for dealing with the impact of contracting on the morale of remaining staff?	_____	_____

Legal

	Yes	No
Is it legal for the district to enter into a contract with a private company in this state?	_____	_____
Will the company be liable for expenses incurred due to legal challenges against its contract with the district?	_____	_____
Does contract language clearly identify the responsibilities for filing reports with governmental entities?	_____	_____
Has the district consulted with its attorney regarding responsibility for the execution of obligations imposed by law such as rights of the handicapped, employee rights to review personnel records, civil rights protection, and due process procedures?	_____	_____
Do the district and its employees have protection from litigation and costs resulting from non-compliance with state and federal regulations and rules?	_____	_____
Will the company indemnify the district (including attorney fees) for added exposure to third-party claims by employees of the contractor and its sub-contractors for any of the following:		
violations of law?	_____	_____
contract breaches?	_____	_____
additional tax liens?	_____	_____
acts of omission and commission?	_____	_____

	Yes	*No*
Is the district protected from liability for the company's acts after the termination of the contract?	_____	_____
Are competitive bidding procedures identified?	_____	_____
Is the company required to disclose all of the commitments and obligations that it makes in its implementation of the contract in the district?	_____	_____
Does the contract identify under what conditions the parties may declare a breach of contract?	_____	_____
Is contract language specific enough to overcome claims that the district remains the employer or is a joint employer?	_____	_____
Is the privatization contract consistent with the district's collective bargaining agreements?	_____	_____

Contractual Items: Samples for the Practitioner

This section is intended to suggest a non-exhaustive set of sample statements that might be rewritten as contractual language with an Education Management Organization (EMO). An EMO contract is presented because such an agreement would necessarily deal with some especially complex questions and the most inclusive list of items (e.g., curriculum, instruction, student achievement, etc.) of any privatization document.

Since the authors believe that good contractual relationships are situational, the following items are provided only as a guide. A district *must consult its own legal advisors* to determine whether a particular example is appropriate, specific, or adequately broad for the particular requirements of that district. In those cases where we believe the suggested language may not be self-explanatory, we include a "Note of explanation."

The following sample contract proposals assume a long-term contract.

ACCESS TO RECORDS

The access of district staff, parents, and students to student records will be guided by district policy in accordance with state and federal law.

ACCREDITATION

The company will assure that the district's schools will annually achieve the highest level accreditation based on the then current standards established by accrediting governmental, regional, and university agencies.

Note of explanation: We suggest here that when EMOs are responsible for instruction and/or curriculum in an environment where accreditation is available, the responsibility for meeting such standards be contractually identified.

ADDITIONAL CHARGES

The company will submit in writing by certified mail to the administration any charges it deems additional to the specifications contained in the company's original proposal. The board of education will have thirty days to accept or deny any additional charges. The board is entitled to set a ceiling on any expense that the administration may approve without board approval. Further, the board may seek alternate bids from additional contractors if the item in question was not contained in the original bid by the contractor.

Note of explanation: On occasion, neither the company nor the district anticipates an expense for which both agree the district is financially responsible. This may occur if the item was not contained within the specifications on which the contractor bid (e.g., a bus garage lift in need of repair). However, the board should have the option to seek competitive bids for any items not contained in the contractor's original bid.

ASSUMED COSTS

The company will provide a schedule of costs for which the company has committed or becomes obligated and which the district may assume at its discretion upon termination of the contract. The district will be provided disclosure of all terms prior to the company's entry into long-term obligations for which the district becomes liable. This schedule shall include but will not be limited to leases or other financing vehicles, technology-related personnel support, maintenance and upgrade costs, software licenses or service agreements, etc.

Note of explanation: It is possible that the company may enter into a lease/purchase or some other financial arrangement that is not completed by the time the company's contract is terminated. The district should seek to control the decision whether to continue the lease arrangement or to "walk away from it."

BREADTH OF CURRICULUM

The district's curriculum (i.e., art, music, P.E., athletics, technology education, foreign language, etc.) will be maintained at no less than its current level of offerings.

BUDGET DEVELOPMENT

The board of education shall retain the right to develop all elements of the district's budget. The district will seek advice from the company regarding budgetary items that affect the company's activities within the district.

Note of explanation: Although it is to the EMO's economic benefit to establish the budget and control revenues and expenditures, the district's best interests will be served when the board controls the budget. This may be one of the major contentious issues during board/contractor negotiations.

CAPITAL INVESTMENTS

The cost, date of acquisition, and estimated useful life of each purchase made by the company shall be recorded and shared with the district. These costs will be paid for by the company directly, as well as all personnel support, maintenance, and upgrade costs. No capital expenditure that has terms which exceed the contract term may be made without the district's approval.

Note of explanation: As the company implements the contract, it may want to make a capital expenditure that will have implications for the district's budget beyond the term of the contract; e.g., maintenance contracts, utility and custodial costs for new facilities, etc. It is best that the board control all future obligations.

CERTIFICATION

Company employees providing instructional service may be required to possess appropriate certification and meet other standards at the board's discretion.

COLLECTIVE BARGAINING

The company will not seek to implement any changes to the wages, hours, or other working conditions of district employees subject to a collective bargaining agreement, unless pursuant to an agreement with the applicable union, or as otherwise allowed by contract or law. The company will assume full responsibility for acting in accordance with these obligations.

COMPENSATION

Compensation paid to the company will be based upon a percentage of the difference between previous costs of managing the district's programs in a base year and actual annual costs incurred under the company's management. A compensation payment schedule will be mutually determined by the parties to the contract.

Note of explanation: Probably the most desirable financial arrangement for the EMO is to receive the total district revenue and keep whatever is left after running the district. However, the district might attempt to establish the prior cost of a district function and agree to a predetermined percentage it will give to the company from the savings realized by the company's management of that function. The district might consider a minimum period (e.g., quarterly) for each period.

COMPETITIVE BIDDING

All state and local competitive bidding requirements, i.e., those pertaining to the purchase of supplies, materials, and equipment, as well as those regarding the repair, renovation, and/or construction of buildings will be adhered to by the company, its affiliates, and subcontractors, as if those purchases were being made by the district.

Note of explanation: Many states require very specific purchasing procedures for school districts that cannot be waived even when subcontracting the service to a private company.

CONTRACT MONITORING

The district will have reasonable access to all company records and performance ratings that relate to the company's activity within the district. The company will submit progress reports to the administration on a schedule established by the district and/or with reasonable notice.

CONTROL OF REVENUES

Federal, state, and local revenue, including the sale of district assets and loan proceeds, shall remain in district control. These funds shall be deposited in the district's bank accounts and not be transferred to the company. Under no circumstances will the company be considered a trustee for such funds.

CRIMINAL CHECKS AND DRUG TESTING

The company's employees and others retained by the company to perform services within the district may be required to submit to criminal history checks and testing for the use of illicit drugs as determined by the district or as required by state or federal law.

CURRICULUM LEADERSHIP

The company will annually assign the minimum equivalent of [insert number] full time curriculum specialists to implement the curriculum improvement cycle.

Note of explanation: When the EMO is responsible for providing curriculum leadership, the board may wish to establish the level of professional resources it requires the company to provide. This requirement would be in addition to contract language that requires student learning results.

CURRICULUM MANDATES

The company will be required to comply with all state and national mandates for instruction and curriculum.

DISCLOSURE

In order to monitor the activities of the company, the company will make a full, written disclosure of all commitments and obligations that it incurs in order to achieve the terms contained in the agreement between it and the district within thirty days of the date on which the company enters into such obligations.

EMPLOYEE ASSIGNMENT

Company employees may have their placement and continued assignment within the district subject to the board's approval.

ERRORS AND OMISSIONS

The company will provide appropriate bonds and other security instruments to protect the district and its employees throughout the term of its agreement with the company and for any matter that continues or arises after termination of the contract if it relates to acts or omissions by company employees during the contract term.

EVALUATION OF INSTRUCTION

A longitudinal study by a third party company or institution of the board of education's selection will be conducted to determine the products and results of privatizing. Funding for the evaluation will be considered as normal operating expense to be paid by the company, unless funded by outside agencies and/or foundations. The following domains will be included in the evaluation of the outcomes of the company's efforts:

- students' academic performance and attitudes
- instruction, including curriculum and instructional quality
- parent and community satisfaction with the district's educational program (either children's work, the schools' work, or both)
- the management and operation of the schools, including both instructional and non-instructional elements
- the costs of education in the district and the relation between benefits and costs

EXCESS COSTS

All operating costs up to a certain sum will be paid by the district with its normally appropriated funds and for the activity agreed to by the parties. The company will bear the responsibility for any excess costs except for those costs that are the result of the district's prior obligations that were not disclosed.

Note of explanation: The company will contract to perform specific functions for a fixed price. The district should be protected from cost overruns.

EXTERNAL AUDIT

The company's district operations, as well as those of its affiliates and subcontractors, will be subject to reasonable audits, in accordance with current and accepted industry standards, scheduled by district agents to assure compliance with the contract and the district's legal obligations.

INDEMNIFICATION

The company will indemnify (including reasonable attorney fees) the district for any violations of local ordinances or state and federal law, as well as contract breaches and any and all tax liens, and all other liabilities resulting from acts or omissions of the company's agents, employees, or those of its affiliates and/or subcontractors and third parties. The company will maintain its liability after termination of the contract for those actions that took place while the contract was in force.

INDEPENDENT EVALUATION

The school district reserves the right to gather its own data in pursuit of evaluating the services provided under the contract. These data will not be limited to personnel and management performance and may be in addition to company collected data.

LITIGATION

The cost of defending the district against litigation arising from the contract with the company or for worker's compensation or other indemnifications will be borne by the company. (No district funds may be used for this purpose.)

MEDIATION

Those disputes between the parties to this contract that arise out of interpretation of contractual items will first be submitted to a panel of three mutually agreed-to mediators. The cost of such mediation will be borne equally by the district and the company. If agreement is not reached through the mediation process, either party will be free to seek other remedies, including through the court system.

OPERATIONAL COSTS

All funds to pay for company promised improvements (additional teachers, athletic subsidies, etc.) will be transferred to the district's accounts by the company thirty days prior to the commencement of the contractual obligations for these expenses.

Note of explanation: When the company promises program or service upgrades for which it will make full expenditure at the outset, the board should require receipt of any funds that the company's actions obligate the district to subsequently pay. For example, the district should receive funds to pay total costs for hiring staff to teach foreign languages prior to signing contracts for the service.

OWNERSHIP

All items purchased with district funds will be deemed district property.

PERFORMANCE BOND

A performance bond will be purchased by the company at its sole cost and expense that covers any obligation that the company has incurred as a result of its proposal to the district. A copy of the performance bond will be provided to the district prior to the commencement of the contract. The bond may be executed by the district in the event that the company withdraws from its obligations for any reason and/or defaults on any portion of its commitment to the contract term. The performance bond will cover at a minimum:

- eighteen months of salaries for teachers hired with company funds (If fewer than eighteen months remain on the contract, the length of time remaining shall be substituted.)
- unemployment and all other costs, including legal costs, associated with the layoff of those staff used to implement the contract
- eighteen months of lease payments on all technology (If fewer

than eighteen months remain on the contract, the length of time remaining shall be substituted.)

- completion of the longitudinal evaluation
- all monies received from the district, or on behalf of the district, but not expended on the district's behalf
- all expenses for restoring to full district usability the information, student records, budgeting data, etc. critical to the district's effective management of its affairs

The performance bond will stipulate that an interim payment stream of 1/12 of the sum of the above costs will be made to the district per month with any excess paid to be refunded.

Note of explanation: Similar to other contract items in this appendix, examples are not all-inclusive nor are the suggested time periods appropriate to every situation.

REVENUE

Revenue that is realized in excess of those revenues that existed at the time the contract was executed will not be included in the calculation of the company's profit.

Note of explanation: It is important that the district maintain control over its revenue stream. This especially pertains to contracts that permit the company to keep all the revenue left after providing service. As an example, it is desirable to have a contractual agreement specifying which party financially benefits from any increase in the state allotment for transportation.

SPECIAL EDUCATION

Special education programs will be executed in compliance with all state and federal regulations. A full continuum of programs will be maintained consistent with federal and state mandates or guidelines. The members of the Individualized Educational Placement Committee will continue to make the determination of appropriate programs, services, and placement. All parental procedural safeguards will be observed. The company will be responsible to defend any and all charges made against the special education delivery system arising as a result of its contract with the district.

STUDENT ACHIEVEMENT

The company's leadership of the district's curriculum and instruction will result in the following gains for students beginning in the third year of the contract:

- All general education students will read at or above grade level by the end of the 2nd grade and at or above grade level thereafter.
- Beginning in the year 2000, district students, as a group, will demonstrate a 10 percent improvement above 1997 percentiles, and will thereafter maintain the improvement on the following standards:
    (1) All standardized test scores (e.g., State Minimal Standards Tests, SRA, ACT, PSAT, CTBS) and other tests identified by the independent agency conducting the evaluation of the district's privatizing efforts
    (2) Retention rates, graduation rates, advanced placement, advanced college credits, success on the job, and success in rates of entry into post-secondary programs and their completion
- Beginning with the graduating class of 2000, all high school graduates will successfully complete three years of high school mathematics and three years of high school science.

Note of explanation: We again emphasize the suggestive nature of all the items contained in this appendix. Districts will need to tailor to their own circumstances the contractual items that express the standards for judging student achievement.

TRANSFER OF EQUIPMENT

Title to all equipment transferred to the company will be approved by the board of education in accordance with the board's pre-existing or future policy.

For-Profit Firms Serving Education

The following list of for-profit firms is only suggestive of the very large and growing number of private firms that provide direct and management services, instructional programming, non-instructional services, and technology services to the education marketplace. Most of the named companies are contained in *The School Administrator* and *Mackinac Center* publications. For current and extensive directories of for-profit firms serving the education marketplace, contact the American Association of Educators in Private Practice, AAEPP, N7425 Switzke Road, Watertown, WI 53094, (800) 252-3280; and the Education Industry Directory, P.O. Box 1819, St. Cloud, MN 56302, (320) 251-8323.

EDUCATIONAL MANAGEMENT ORGANIZATIONS

Alternative Public Schools, Inc.
28 White Bridge Rd.
 Suite 311
Nashville, TN 37205
(615) 356-6975

Edison Project
529 Fifth Avenue, 12th floor
New York, NY 10017
(212) 309-1600

Education Alternatives, Inc.
7900 Xerxes Ave. South
Minneapolis, MN 55431
(612) 885-5572

Public Strategies Group, Inc.
275 East 4th Street, Suite 710
St. Paul, MN 55101-1628
(612) 227-9774

Roy Jorgensen Associates, Inc.
P.O. Box 70
Buckeystown, MD 21717
(800) 638-5930

155

Sabis School Network
6385 Beach Road
Eden Prairie, MN 55344
(612) 941-3500

Sylvan Learning Systems
9135 Guilford Road
Columbia, MD 21046
(410) 880-0889

EDUCATIONAL SERVICES

Berlitz Jr.
125 Main St.
Westport, CT 06880
(800) 528-7929

Designs for Learning
2550 University Ave. W.
Suite 347N
St. Paul, MN 55114-1052
(612) 645-0200

DiaLogos International
   Corporation
5104 Oak Park Rd.
Raleigh, NC 27612
(910) 782-2630

Flam & Associates, Consultants
28786 Rockledge Dr.
Farmington Hills, MI 48334-1758
(810) 626-8062

Futurekids
5777 W. Century Blvd., Suite 1555
Los Angeles, CA 90045-5678
(310) 337-7006

Huntington Learning Centers
496 Kinderkamack Road
Oradell, NJ 07649
(201) 261-8400

Language Odyssey
401 North Michigan Ave.
Chicago, IL 60611
(800) 259-0033

Ombudsman Educational
   Services, Ltd.
1585 North Milwaukee Ave.
Libertyville, IL 60048
(800) 833-9235

Options for Youth, Inc.
2529 Foothill Blvd., Suite 1
LaCrescenta, CA 91214-3521
(818) 542-3555

Science Encounters
4401 East West Highway
Suite 300
Bethesda, MD 20814
(301) 718-0808

NON-INSTRUCTIONAL SERVICES

ARA Services, School Division
1101 Market St., 20th Floor
Philadelphia, PA 19107
(800) 328-5200

Durham Transportation, Inc.
9171 Capital of Texas Hwy. North
Travis Bldg., Suite 200
Austin, TX 78759-7252
(512) 343-6292

Johnson Controls World
Services, Inc.
7315 North Atlantic Ave.
Cape Canaveral, FL 32920-3792
(407) 784-7368

Laidlaw Transit
7501 S. Quincy, Suite L
Willowbrook, IL 60521
(708) 887-0134

Marriott International, Inc.
One Marriott Drive
Washington, D.C. 20058
(301) 380-9000

Mayflower Contract Services
5360 College Blvd.
Shawnee Mission, KS 66207
(913) 345-1986

National Big Bus Council
1819 West Pershing Road
Chicago, IL 60609
(312) 535-7740

National School Bus
Service, Inc.
18-4 East Dundee Road
Barrington, IL 60010
(708) 382-0525

Preferred Meal Systems
1672 Reynolds Avenue
Irvine, CA 92714
(714) 770-5590

Ryder Student Transportation
Services
P.O. Box 020816
Miami, FL 33102-0816
(800) 648-7787

Service Master
1 Service Master Way
Downer's Grove, IL 60515
(800) 333-6678

The Wackenhut Corporation
1500 San Remo Avenue
Coral Gables, FL 33146-3009
(305) 666-5656

Wilkerson & Associates, P.C.
19627 Grand River
Detroit, MI 48223
(313) 532-2660

TECHNOLOGY

American Management
Systems, Inc.
4050 Legato Road
Fairfax, VA 22033
(703) 267-8000

Apple Computer, Inc.
1 Infinite Loop
Cupertino, CA 95014-2084
(408) 996-1010

Autodesk, Inc.
2320 Marinship Wy.
Sausalito, CA 94965
(800) 964-6432

Bolt Beranek and Newman, Inc.
150 Cambridge Park Drive
Cambridge, MA 02140
(617) 873-3897

Broderbund Software, Inc.
500 Redwood Blvd.
P.O. Box 6121
Novato, CA 94948-6121
(415) 382-4449

Computer Curriculum Corp.
1287 Lawrence Station Rd.
Sunnyvale, CA 94089
(408) 541-3951

Edunetics Corporation
1600 Wilson Blvd. Suite 710
Arlington, VA 22209-2505
(703) 243-2602

Eduquest
411 Northside Parkway
Atlanta, GA 30327
(404) 238-2000

Jostens Learning
6170 Cornerstone Ct.
San Diego, CA 92121
(800) 521-8538

Minnesota Educational
  Computing Consortium (MECC)
6160 Summit Dr. North
Minneapolis, MN 55430-4003
(612) 569-1500

National Computer Systems, Inc.
11000 Prairie Lakes Drive
Eden Prairie, MN 55344
(612) 829-3000

EDUCATION INDUSTRY—COMPANY CLASSIFICATIONS

Listed below are the industry classifications of most companies that provide private service to public education. This division is provided to help the reader better understand the hierarchy of available companies in the education industry. It follows closely the sector analysis provided within the *The Education Industry Directory* which is currently the most complete of its kind.

I.   Education Management Organizations (EMOs)
    A. Total Management
        1. Proprietary K–12 Schools
        2. Contract Management of K–12 Schools
        3. Proprietary Postsecondary Schools
    B. Special Programs
        1. Preschools/Child Care Centers

      2. At Risk Youth

      3. Foreign Language

      4. Special Subject/Activities

II. Educational Services

    A. Consultants/Curriculum Designers

    B. Learning Centers

    C. Training and Development

    D. Other Educational Services

III. Educational Products

    A. Publishing

    B. Technology

    C. Educational Materials

    D. School Supplies

IV. Non-Instructional Services

    A. Facility Management

    B. Finance

    C. Food Service

    D. Health Care

    E. Information Management

    F. Security

    G. Transportation

Asset Management An active process for increasing the value of existing assets by such methods as investing cash surpluses, selling or leasing unused equipment, and renting facilities for use during non-school hours.

Bid Bond A bond of a specific denomination that is forfeited to the district if the contractor fails to carry out the terms and conditions of the bid or proposal that is accepted. Provides full protection for the district in case a bidder fails to initiate a contract that has been awarded. Can be prohibitively expensive for relatively new firms without a track record and thereby reduce the number of viable bidders.

Budget Targeting A method of forcing cost savings by establishing financial targets for the delivery of a service and involving employees in methods for meeting those targets.

Charter School A public school operated with public funds and conforming to the financial and academic reporting systems for all public schools but initiated and managed by an entity other than a publicly elected board of education.

Construction Management A technique for managing construction projects that employs a firm at a fixed fee to coordinate the various components of the project and to supervise bidding of all subcontracts. This methodology eliminates the role of the general contractor, who may have a tendency to make compromises that will reduce quality in order to maximize profit.

Contracting for Core Services A contract with a business, university, or other entity to provide a single academic program or manage the total educational program of a school or entire district.

Contracting for Support Services   A contract with a business or other entity to provide one or more non-instructional functions for the district.

Direct Costs   Those costs that are completely attributed to a single function, service, or activity; for example, bus driver salaries pay for only one function, the operation of buses.

Due Diligence   The intensive, systematic investigation of an organization, private or public, which reveals whether the entity can perform as expected and/or as it claims.

Education Industry Directory   A publication that provides business information about companies offering products or services to public education. It is probably the most readily available single source of information for districts looking at privatizing for the first time.

Education Industry Index (EI Index)   A publication that tracks the efforts of all businesses that provide programs, products and services to the P–12 education market.

Education Industry Report   A monthly bulletin that reports on private sector activity in education.

Education Management Organization (EMO)   A term used to describe a private sector company that provides management to the total operation of a school or a school district.

Indirect Cost   Costs that are expended to support more than one function, service, or activity and which must be prorated to determine the proportion attributable to any one function or service; e.g., a payroll department that provides services to many different units within the organization.

Interdistrict Agreements   A voluntary agreement among several school districts to coordinate efforts and thereby reduce the costs for each. An example would be two small districts building a bus service garage to serve both districts.

Invitation to Bid (ITB)   A public statement inviting vendors to offer the lowest bid possible to provide a product or products that meet bid specifications. Most often used when purchasing materials and equipment, especially when price will be the key criterion for selecting a vendor.

Magnet School A public school that serves students from multiple attendance boundaries who are interested in the particular focus of the school (e.g., science, art, mathematics, music, Black Studies, etc.)

Opportunity Costs The loss of ability to use district property or equipment for more valuable purposes or to increase revenue from the sale, lease, or rental of such properties, which are currently devoted to a necessary function of the district.

Outsourcing The assignment of specific work to a third party for a specific length of time with an agreed-upon price for an expected service level. Refers essentially to the practice of contracting out part of the total core operation or a support service.

Performance Bond A bond written by an insurance company that guarantees that work undertaken by a contractor will be completed. If the contractor is unable to carry out the contract for its full term, or all of its conditions, the insurance company will take over the responsibility for fulfilling the contract at no additional cost to the district.

Private Practice Teachers Individual teachers or groups of teachers who contract directly with school districts, with companies, or with parents to provide instructional services to students. Many private practice teachers are members of the American Association of Educators in Private Practice (AAEPP).

Privatization The process of turning over to private companies the programs, services, and sometimes properties previously considered the responsibility of a government agency.

Public-Private Partnerships A relationship between a governmental agency and one or more privately held companies to offer one or more programs or services to the public, often programs or services previously offered exclusively by the government body. Such partnerships may cover a wide range of agreements, such as company sponsored satellite schools, mentors in the workplace, storytellers in the classroom, etc.

Request for Proposals (RFP) A public statement inviting vendors to offer a particular service that includes the vendor's conditions and specifications upon which the offer is based. Often used when factors other than low price are the chief criteria for selecting a contractor.

SWOT Analysis An analysis of the strengths, weaknesses, opportunities, and threats involved in a particular situation or action and that is used to estimate the probable results of a contemplated action.

Transitional Costs Those additional expenses that arise from facilitating the transition from a public provided to a privately provided function, service, or activity.

Vouchers In education, a voucher is an instrument used for the transfer of public funds to a person, program, school, or business that educates students in a setting other than a public school.

REFERENCES

Abramson, P. 1993. The vending machine. *American School and University*. 66: 44.

American Association of School Administrators. 1995. Private firms in the public school marketplace. *The School Administrator*. 52: 8–9.

American Federation of Teachers. 1994. *The private management of public schools: An analysis of the EAI experience in Baltimore*. Washington, D.C.: Author.

Amprey, W. Telephone conversation with S. Flam, 22 February 1994.

Anderson, H. & The Yankee Group. 1995. Innovations in outsourcing. *Forbes Advertising Supplement*. October 23.

Archer, J. 1996. Neb. lawmakers back new caps on property taxes, *Education Week,* 17 April 1996, p. 11.

Atherton, C. & Windsor, D. 1987. Privatizaton of urban services. In *Entrepreneurship and the privatization of government,* ed. C. A. Kent, 81–99. New York: Quorum Books.

Ascher, K. 1991. The business of local government. In *Privatization: The provision of public services by the private sector,* ed. R. L. Kemp, 297–304. Jefferson, NC: McFarland & Co.

Bailey, R. W. 1991. Uses and misuses. In *Privatization: The provision of public services by the private sector,* ed. R. L. Kemp, 87–96. Jefferson, NC: McFarland & Co.

Beales, J. 1994. *Doing more with less: Competitive contracting for school support services.* Midland, MI: Mackinac Center for Public Policy/Reason Foundation.

Beales, J. 1995. *Teacher, Inc.: A private practice option for educators.* Midland, MI: Mackinac Center for Public Policy/Reason Foundation.

Beales, J. & O'Leary, J. 1994. *Making schools work: Contracting options for better management.* Midland, MI: Mackinac Center for Public Policy/Reason Foundation.

Bennett, D. A. 1991.The centennial essay. *The American School Board Journal*, 178, 10: 35–37.

Berliner, D. & Biddle, B. 1995. *The manufactured crisis: Myths, fraud, and the attacks on America's public schools.* Reading, MA: Addison Wesley.

Blumenfeld, S. 1981. *Is public education necessary.* Old Greenwich, CT: Devin Adair.

Borden, K. & Rauchut, E. A. 1996. Choice: Making even good schools better. *Education Week,* April 17, pp. 20, 23.

Carlson, R. V. & Awkerman, G. eds. 1991. *Educational planning: Concepts, strategies, practices.* White Plains, NY: Longman.

Center on National Education Policy. 1996. *Do we still need public schools?* Bloomington, IN: Phi Delta Kappa.

Doyle, D. 1994. The role of private sector management in public education. *Phi Delta Kappan,* 76: 128–132.

Edney, J. & O'Neill, R. 1990. Finding the hidden costs, *Thrust for Educational Leadership.* 20:56–59.

Education Commission of the States 1992. *Building private sector and community support.* Denver, CO: Author.

Finkel, K. 1991. The true cost of student transportation. *School and College,* September, quoted in Janet R. Beales and John O'Leary, *Making schools work: Contracting options for better management* (Midland, MI: Mackinac Center for Public Policy/Reason Foundation, January 1994), p. 7.

Florestano, P. J. 1985. Considerations for the future of privatization. *Urban Resources.* 2, 4: 6–9.

Glazer, N. 1983. The future under tuition tax credits. In *Public dollars for private schools: The case of tuition tax credits,* eds. A. T. Jones and H. Levin, 87–100. Philadelphia: Temple University Press.

Goldberg, M. 1995. Education in Baltimore: An interview with Mayor Kurt Schmoke. *Phi Delta Kappan,* 77: 234–237.

Gormley, W. T., ed. 1991. *Privatization and its alternatives.* Madison, WI: University of Wisconsin Press.

Hatry, H. 1991. Problems. In *Privatization: The provision of public services by the private sector,* ed. R. L. Kemp, 262–266. Jefferson, NC: McFarland & Co.

Herzberg, F., Mausner, B., & Snyderman, B. B. 1959. *The motivation to work.* New York, NY: Wiley and Sons.

High, J. & Ellig, J. 1988. In *The theory of market failure: A critical examination,* ed. Tyler Cowen, 361–382. Fairfax, VA: George Mason University Press.

Hilke, J. n.d. *Cost savings from privatization: A compilation of study findings.* Midland, MI: Mackinac Center for Public Policy/Reason Foundation.

Houston, P. 1994. Making watches or making music. *Phi Delta Kappan,* 76: 133–135.

Johnson, P. 1983. *Modern times: The world from the twenties to the eighties.* New York: Harper and Row.

Kemp, R. L. ed. 1991. *Privatization: The provision of public services by the private sector.* Jefferson, NC: McFarland & Co.

Kent, C. A., ed. 1987. *Entrepreneurship and the privatization of government.* New York, NY: Quorum Books.

Kolderie, T. and Hauer, J. Contracting as an approach to public management. In *Privatization: The provision of public services by the private sector,* ed. R. L. Kemp 87–96. Jefferson, NC: McFarland & Co.

Lewis, A. 1995. An atomized America. *New York Times,* December 18, 1995, Editorial page.

Lieberman, M. 1989. *Privatization and educational choice.* New York: St. Martin's Press.

Lieberman, M.1993. Public education: An autopsy. Cambridge, MA: Harvard University Press.

Lieberman, M. 1995. Restoring school board options on contracting out. *Briefings,* 20 November, 1995. Sacramento, CA: The Claremont Institute.

Lipset, S. M. & Schneider, W. 1983. *The confidence gap.* New York: Free Press.

Marcel, B. 1994. *Cost study considerations when contracting for transportation services.* Unpublished Master's Degree Project, Eastern Michigan University, May, 1994.

Martin, L. n.d. *How to compare costs between in-house and contracted services.* Midland, MI: Mackinac Center for Public Policy/Reason Foundation.

McGriff, D. 1995. Lighting the way to systemic reform: The Edison Project launches its version of a public-private partnership. *The School Administrator,* 52: 14–17, 19.

McLaughlin, J. M., ed. 1996. The teachers' unions: The 800 pound gorilla? *The Education Industry Report,* St. Cloud, MN, 4, 1: 1.

Miller, L. 1995. Profiting from experience. *Education Week,* 8 November, 1995, pp. 22–29.

Murphy, J. 1996. Privatization policy: Framing the school reform debate. Invited address at the annual meeting of the American Educational Research Association, New York City, April, 1996.

Nanus, B. 1995. *Visionary leadership.* San Francisco, CA: Jossey-Bass.

National Advisory Commission on Civil Disorders. 1968. *Report.* Washington, D.C.: GPO.

National Education Association. 1995a. *Contracting out: Strategies for fighting back.* Washington, D.C.: Author.

National Education Association. 1995b. *The people's cause: Mobilizing for public education.* Washington, D.C.: Author.

National School Boards Association. 1995a. *Guidelines for contracting with private providers for educational services.* Alexandria, VA: Author.

National School Boards Association. 1995b. *Private options for public schools: Ways public schools are exploring privatization.* Alexandria, VA: Author.

Odden, A. 1996. Productive discussions about the education dollar. *Education Week,* February 7, 37–41.

O'Leary, J. & Beales, J. R. 1994. P.S., INC. *Reason* (June) pp. 37–41.

Osborne, D. & Gaebler, T. 1992. *Reinventing government.* Reading, MA: Addison Wesley Publishing Co.

Pack, J. R. 1991. The opportunities and constraints of privatization. In *Privatization and its alternatives,* ed. W. T. Gormley, 281–306. Madison, WI: University of Wisconsin Press.

Peters, T. 1995. Whence comes innovation. *Forbes ASAP,* August, 132, 130.

Pirie, M. 1988. *Privatization.* London: Wildwood House Ltd.

Private firms in the public marketplace. 1995. *The School Administrator,* August, 8, 9.

Private Sector Tack Force on Management and Productivity. 1996. *Reviews on transportation, facilities, human resources, food service, management information systems.* Philadelphia, PA: School District of Philadelphia.

Rehfuss, J. 1989. *Contracting out in government.* San Francisco, CA: Jossey-Bass.

Report of the President's Commission on Privatization. 1987. *Privatization: Toward more effective government.* Washington, D.C.: Superintendent of Documents.

Roy, R. 1995. *Privatization in Pinckney.* Presentation to the Michigan Association of School Administrators, January 14, 1995, Dearborn, MI.

Savas, E. S. 1987. *Privatization: The key to better government.* Chatham, NJ: Chatham House Publishers, Inc.

Schmidt, P. Private enterprise. *Education Week,* 25 May 1994, pp. 27–30.

Schneider, J. & Houston, P. 1993. *Exploding the myths: Another round in the education debate.* Arlington, VA: American Association of Educational Service Agencies.

School Bus Fleet. January, 1994. *Pupil transportation and data statistics,* 40, 1: 29–36.

Starn, P. 1991. The case for skepticism. In *Privatization and its alternatives,* ed. W. T. Gormley, 25–36. Madison, WI: University of Wisconsin Press.

Taebel, D. and Brenner, C. 1994. *Privatizing public education: The Texas experience.* Arlington, TX: University of Texas School of Urban and Public Affairs.

Taggart, C. 1990. Accounting for costs. In *School Transportation,* a supplement to *The American School Board Journal.* 177: A1–A14.

Touche Ross. 1987. *Privatization in America: An opinion survey of city and county governments on their use of privatization and their infrastructure needs.* Washington, D.C.: Author.

U. S. Department of Transportation National Highway Traffic Safety Administration. 1992. *Traffic Safety Facts 1992.* Washington D.C.: National Center for Statistics and Analysis.

Wagner, J. C. ed. 1996. *The education industry directory 1996.* Boston, MA: EduVentures.

Winslow, F. E. 1991. The politics of advocacy. In *Privatization: The provision of public services by the private sector,* ed. R. L. Kemp, 132–142. Jefferson, NC: McFarland & Co.

Samuel Flam served for twelve years as a public school teacher, counselor, and school administrator in an urban school district before joining the staff of the Michigan/Ohio Regional Educational Laboratory as a leader in the Teacher Behavior Improvement Project. He served the next twenty years in a suburban school district as the Director of Secondary Education, Deputy Superintendent, and Chief Executive. Since retiring from the superintendency in 1988, Dr. Flam has been providing consulting services in organizational development to local and regional school districts; the Michigan Department of Education; colleges and universities; regional, state and federal government agencies; and private industry. Dr. Flam has taught at the graduate level at Oakland University, and he is currently an Adjunct Staff member in Wayne State University's College of Education.

He has shared his experiences and insights through professional journal articles, U.S. Department of Education documents, a local newspaper column, guest lectures at Michigan colleges and universities, professional conference presentations, and a periodic cable television program.

William G. Keane served for twenty-three years as a public school superintendent. During the first nine years of that period, he served as the Chief Executive of the Berkley Public Schools in Berkley, Michigan. From 1980 to 1994, he was superintendent of Oakland Schools, a service agency serving twenty-eight local school districts and 170,000 public school students in Oakland County, Michigan. Prior to these superintendencies, he served as ajunior high school and high school English teacher in New York, a director of secondary education in Michigan, and assistant superintendent of curriculum and instruction for the Woodbridge, New Jersey, Public Schools. He is now Associate Professor in the Department of Curriculum, Instruction, and Leadership at Oakland University in Rochester, Michigan, where, in addition to his teaching duties, he is director for the Education Specialist degree program.

His articles have appeared in many education journals, including *The American School Board Journal, The School Administrator, ERS Spectrum, The Record,* and other publications. In 1996, Corwin Press published his book *Win/Win or Else: Collective Bargaining in an Age of Public Discontent.*